Jill Jensen appeared in two
full-length library productions.
She is a professional actress
and works on the staff of a
communications company.

Jean Jacobson serves on the
Racine (WI) County Board,
and in that capacity hosted
the library's documentary
about the Festival Hall/
Marina project.

CHEAP SHOTS
VIDEO PRODUCTION
FOR NONPROFITS

by

Pat Kardas

The Scarecrow Press, Inc.
Metuchen, N.J., & London
1993

British Library Cataloguing-in-Publication data available

Library of Congress Cataloging-in-Publication Data

Kardas, Pat, 1933-
    Cheap shots : video production for nonprofits / by Pat Kardas.
       p.   cm.
    Includes bibliographical references.
    ISBN 0-8108-2648-8 (alk. paper)
    1. Video recordings--Production and direction.   I. Title.
PN1992.75.K29 1993
791.45'0232--dc20   92-40042

This book is dedicated to Pete Rasmussen, the video wizard whose enthusiasm proved to be catching. Thanks, Pete.

TABLE OF CONTENTS

ACKNOWLEDGMENTS

I wish to acknowledge the assistance of Ellen Snyder, Reference Librarian, and Barry Johnson, Video Cameraman/Editor, Racine Public Library; to Saul Amdursky, Director, Kalamazoo Public Library, special thanks for his advice and encouragement; and maternal gratitude to my son, Eric Kralicek, for his technical assistance with maddening computer glitches.

I must also acknowledge my most important reasons for wanting to preserve the past and instruct the future: my five grandchildren, Jamie, Stacey, Paul, Alyssa and Andrew.

FOREWORD

The center of everyone's universe is someplace different. Public libraries are unique because they can be a part of that center for disparate individuals. The reason libraries can serve a wide variety of individuals is that successful libraries are about information — information that can be delivered in a variety of formats, including video.

Video is the breakthrough medium of this generation for libraries. Video use can be very similar to print, that is, it can be used to entertain, educate, promote and increase available information. Video can also target specific audiences by age, interest, or ability level. Unlike print, video is comparatively inexpensive to obtain, maintain and produce. Video, because of its visual nature, differs substantially from print in its accessibility.

The video revolution in libraries attests to the validity of a well-known Chinese proverb, "one picture is worth more than ten thousand words."

Ms. Kardas knows this first hand. She worked for nearly a decade at Racine Public Library developing effective and entertaining videos. Most impressive was her ability to relate video production to community activities and needs.

I had the opportunity to work on two video projects with Ms. Kardas. One was enormously successful from both an administrative and end-user point of view while the other . . . was a learning experience.

Racine Public Library, under the leadership of its Director, Jack Le Seur, began a video collection in 1981 in response to an anonymous donation of several thousand dollars. This was at a time when video rental shops were comparatively unique, carried only feature films, and the bulk of rentals (as much as eighty percent) were "adult " films.

Racine Public Library had a strong and heavily used collection of 16mm films at the time. Videos, especially "nonfiction" and children's nonfeature videos, were either totally unavailable or extremely expensive.

A grant proposal was developed to purchase licenses from vendors, such as Phoenix Films and Films, Inc., that would allow 16mm films already owned by the library to be dubbed onto video. Efforts were concentrated primarily in the area of children's nonfeature films.

Ms. Kardas had to master a Rube Goldberg device called a film chain. This process involved a five shutter 16mm projector, a stationary video camera, a multiplexer, several VCRs, a monitor and a custom designed stand. The cost savings were enormous. For example, the cost of purchasing "The Ransom of Red Chief" on video at that time was $450. A sliding schedule was negotiated with the vendor that charged no more than five dollars per minute for a single copy, and three dollars per minute for three of more copies. The film is 27 minutes long. This resulted in a net savings of between $315 and $369.

This program also promoted levels of library cooperation that had not previously existed in Wisconsin. The dubbing project ultimately involved Kenosha Public Library, the Milwaukee Museum, the Milwaukee Public Library and libraries in Oshkosh and Green Bay. Sixteen millimeter resources were freely shared for dubbing with the result that the Wisconsin public served by these libraries had far more juvenile video available than most areas at an earlier date.

Some programs were more educational than useful.

The first program that Ms. Kardas recorded for the System was a workshop for children's librarians that combined a Halloween makeup workshop with Dorothy Haas' luncheon speech on how to attract authors of juvenile and young adult books as speakers. The resulting tape taught both Ms. Kardas and myself the limitations of the equipment being used, the need to plan a shoot, and the very real potential of video production. The tape also gave new meaning to the term "talking head," and screamed out for a bulk eraser.

Despite occasional failures, the potential for video usage was and is obvious and enormous.

When I worked at another library an opportunity presented itself to install a satellite dish. This video application was used primarily to facilitate video teleconferences. This made the public library more useful to its clientele, provided information in an alternative format, and in some cases provided information well in advance of print. The local fire department asked the library to record the monthly Federal Emergency Management Administration (F.E.M.A.) conferences because many of the subjects covered had not been covered in print.

As an administrator, I remain committed to incorporating the use of video in designing a library's overall service and public relations program because it is effective. My library works closely with Cable Access to provide several hours of programming and information each week. This can be information as simple as a scroll of new titles available at the public library or a video of a program on finances for seniors held at the library. The library is extending its client base and maintaining its status as an important player in the information market in both circumstances.

Every library administrator needs to be concerned with institutional survival. As scrutiny of the public sector becomes increasingly more intense, every tax-based institution needs to be able to strongly justify its programs and existence.

Public libraries that have clearly defined rules and an articulated mission will remain important informational entities to the communities they serve. Society and technology are changing rapidly. Libraries need to anticipate change and be flexible enough to respond to the unexpected.

The incorporation of video production into a library's overall program is productive. Video is a tool that enhances library use, increases library visibility and is cost effective. Additionally, grant funds are often available for creative uses of video. Further, the medium is sufficiently flexible to support virtually any library's mission and the opportunities created to market the library are tremendously improved.

Pat Kardas has written an important book about the uses of video production in a public library setting. Hers is an excellent primer. Her anecdotes provide guidelines, cautions and instruction. Most importantly, she documents how video production helped the Racine Public Library maintain a strong position in the community. Video production has helped the Racine Public Library be a part of the center of the universe of the city it serves.

Saul Amdursky, Director
Kalamazoo Public Library

INTRODUCTION

In 1981 I began producing videotapes for a public library. I had a degree in professional communications, a three-tube camera, a couple of VCRs and portable recorders and more questions than answers.

By the time I left the library in 1989 I had amassed a body of work large enough to serve as a sample, to look back on and judge. Some of it was awful. Some of it was good. But there were some videotapes I produced during that period that gave me a real sense of pride.

In management terms, after an initial investment in equipment, the costs of these productions consisted of employee time and the price of videotape. But the benefits went beyond price. A little talent, a little vision and a lot of hard work can create productions that simply will never be made any other way.

They're not commercial; none of us got rich. They're not quite on a par with PBS documentaries or network news. But they are far better than the "cheap pet tricks" videos perpetrated in prime time, and they can provide a unique, invaluable gift for generations to come.

During a workshop held at Marquette University in those first tentative years of video production, I was given as a handout what was described as a partial listing of nonbroadcast video applications. I've adapted that original list to show you the possibilities that await the acquisition of your first professional camera:

Employee news shows
Motivational tapes for staff and new employees
Documentation of construction, insurance claims and records
New product (or library service) demonstrations and feature
    updates
Repair "how-to's"
Comparison of present and proposed site evaluations
Annual reports
Time lapse photography
High speed video = slow motion playback
Time and motion studies
Security
Reference presentations
Patron feedback

Continuing education
Human resource development
Home study courses
Public relations
Programs and Public Service Announcements
Entertainment
Outplacement assistance: helping job seekers identify sources of information
Multi-language presentations
Slide and film conversion to tape
Computer assisted instruction
Simulation of working conditions
Safety training
Standardization of training techniques for different sites
Potential employee evaluation
Role playing/self evaluation
Role modeling: recording the best person demonstrating a
    desired technique
Teleconferencing
Speaker support
"Instant" video: quickly edited tapes of meetings, outings, etc.
Depositions
New employee orientation
Technological processes
Microwave video between remote sites for employee meetings
Slow scan video via phone lines
Cable system communications using 2-way leased channels
Video records for report writing
Computer graphics
Historical records
Basic skill training
Management development

It's astonishing to see how many of those applications fit our own production history. A quick glance at the "videography" at the end of this book will show you just which items seemed to have been plucked straight from that list. But when we were first starting, it seemed unlikely that we would be doing more than one or two of them.

Another interesting thing is the fact that many of our productions fit more than one application. A quick example would be the dual tapes we made about the pressing need for library expansion,

and the soft sell listing of the benefits of library service; these tapes
worked well by themselves, but they were also intended to be used
as speaker support, so that the person giving a speech could tailor
his or her remarks to the given audience and then let the video fill
in an entertaining and informative part of the presentation. People
who weren't comfortable speaking in public could use it quite
easily as an aid. Those who loved to interact with a crowd found
the tapes worked well as springboards for their own observations
and opinions.

Also, during the course of our video work we were offered the
chance to document certain library functions and have these instructional tapes sold through a distributor to other libraries.
Though the offer was refused due to the potential problems of a
nonprofit entity creating profitable, therefore questionable, library
products, the idea intrigued and excited us. Given the need for tax-
supported institutions to generate more revenue in these lean
times, it might be something that another, more innovative school
or library would like to consider. If you have a "superstar" on your
staff, why not share that expertise with others through taped instructions?

Whatever your strong points, go over that list one more time
and let your imagination go. How many of those ideas would
work well for you? How many of them could be adapted to meet
your own special needs? If you keep your options open, you'll find
more there than you ever expected. I know I did.

In the following chapters, I'll tell you how to determine your audience, what kind of equipment you'll want to buy, how to raise
the money to pay for it, where to find the people who will help you
make professional-level programs for free, and how to put all the
pieces together to achieve what you want to achieve on video. And
then I'll tell you when to stop, which can be an art in itself, as you
will see!

For the most part, whatever discussions of technique I include
will be tied to specific examples of videotapes produced by our
library. I'm making the assumption that the people you'll have
doing this work will be professionals. Before starting in production
work I had years of writing experience and video training at the
college level, while our technician had a degree in video production
and worked for a cable station before joining the library.

Both of us had built connections among the AV community in
Racine, Kenosha and Milwaukee, making it even easier to get the

job done. But we also had many other duties beyond those of video production. It was our abiding interest in and love for the work we were doing that gave us an extra push to complete these projects even when we had to put our own time into them.

Without a staff that really care and an administration that backs them up, you probably won't accomplish a lot. But with a little time, a little talent, and a lot of hard work, you can do wonders. To save the voices, faces and events of the present, to investigate and reveal the humanity of the past and to give insight into heritage are all valid goals for institutions whose purpose is to provide information and education.

My experiences were exceptional for their times, but video has now become so commonplace that more and more libraries, schools and other nonprofits are discovering that video is a tool like no other — an immediate grabber in a world where capturing public attention is harder than ever before.

If you have a message to get across or a story to tell, this is the way to do it. Fast, multidimensional, addressing a variety of audiences and needs, video is a versatile medium. But as the technology gets better, simpler and cheaper, using it becomes more complex; there's a lot of commercially or privately produced videotaped material out there, much of it badly done. You could make the mistake of thinking that anything that's been produced by professionals is somehow automatically "right." Tears still come to my eyes when I recall the tape made by a state historical society showcasing some otherwise interesting material. Unfortunately, the technique they used was to set a camera running in front of a professor lecturing by a chalkboard; they assumed that his occasional gesture towards the chalked information on the board constituted a visual aid.

To help you sidestep such pitfalls and avoid having to reinvent the wheel is the purpose of this book. Piggyback on my experiences. Let my disasters help you avoid yours; above all, when you've read the book, go out and do it right. You'll start out with a guaranteed eight years of experience behind you!

Pat Kardas
Racine, Wisconsin

ONE

Point of View:

Who Is Your Audience,

Anyway?

THE WAY WE WERE

Anyone who ever passed Communications 101 knows that the first question to ask yourself is both the hardest and the easiest to answer: who is your audience? Who are you trying to reach? And what are you trying to say to them?

In this decade, it seems difficult to realize what a shock videotapes created when they appeared on public library shelves. Videos have become commonplace items in schools, libraries and grocery stores. But there's still a slight pause when the concept of libraries producing their own videos is discussed. Most schools have gotten used to the switch from an occasional 16mm film being shown in classrooms to the regular use of video, including video produced in the school, but libraries don't enjoy the narrowly defined list of subjects that schools employ when making their own productions. And anyone who's ever answered to a Board knows by heart the sound of one particular voice (there's always one particular voice on any Board) asking, in less than sibilant tones: *What kinds of videos are you talking about? Who'd want to see that kind of stuff anyway?*

Accept the fact that it's a fair question. If you can't list groups of people who would benefit from what you're spending your time on, then perhaps you'd better step back and reconsider the project. It all comes down to absolute basics. Ask yourself again: who is your audience? Who is it you want to reach? And what is it you have to say to them?

1

When I first began formulating ideas for library productions, the answer seemed obvious. The videotapes we planned to make were intended to benefit the vast majority of people in our own home town, our library patrons. These tapes would showcase local history; we could illustrate arts and crafts as taught by our own local artists and artisans; and we would save for posterity fascinating interviews with and about people and places that mattered in our town.

I sat down and made a list, which went on and on. We in America have a rich and diverse history that varies enough from region to region to make each one unique. Even relatively young American towns like Racine (established about 1834) have valuable resources of architecture, industry, education and ethnic diversity from which to choose. The possibilities were endless. And that, of course, is the problem.

It can take a lot of effort to discover just what it is you really want to do, or even what you can do. Each one of us is starting from square one in our own backyard, but it can be helpful to take note of what's been done in the past and to see what worked — and even more instructive, what didn't. In that vein, let me tell you how it was when the Racine Public Library started to experiment with video production out there in the real world of 1981.

My first attempts at videotaping events were, shall we say, instructional. The equipment was barely out of the boxes; I wasn't even sure how most of it worked. A technician from the company that sold us our basic equipment — camera, VCR and microphone — tagged along to help me set up for my first shoot, which was to be a day-long conference. I discovered in the process of doing it that it really couldn't be done.

The conference was a unique one day program for our Board of Trustees. Each Department Head presented information about the area he/she managed, addressing budgets, changes in procedures, hopes for the future and how different plans affected staff concerns. The purpose of the conference was to orient our trustees at a single meeting so that each of them would know exactly what actions were being proposed, the reasons for them, and the effect these changes would have on the operations of the library.

My charge was to record the proceedings for future trustee orientations. I taped the conference using a single three-tube camera mounted on a stationary tripod. The recorder was not portable; it was a standard VHS stationary recorder. Back then those machines were bulky, heavy pieces of equipment requiring a heavy duty table to support them. The recorder was connected by long, umbilical-like cables to the camera, which was in turn connected by still more cables to the 19-inch monitor we used to check picture quality. As you can imagine, this setup really hindered my movements with the camera and limited possible maneuvering space. It felt very much like being underwater in one of those old-style diving suits, trying to film the ballet-like, but unpredictable movements of schools of fish.

Placement of the participants could not have been worse, from a taping point of view. Twenty-some people were arranged around rectangular tables in a room barely large enough to hold them. Shooting from the outside was awkward; placing the camera inside all that wasted space would have been the best arrangement, but there was no way that the camera, cables, television set and me would all fit into that space — even if I could have reached a power source from there. As it was, I feared for the life of anyone trying to get past my cords, cables and peripherals no matter where I made my stand. I found I was getting tangled up from time to time, myself, and was grateful that the microphone didn't pick up the sound of my voice during those moments.

Trying to move the camera/octopus to a position behind the participants' chairs proved equally impossible. I had to make a snap decision on where to place the camera in order to swivel enough to catch the majority of comments and facial expressions. There was some extra space beyond the meeting room where refreshments were laid out, and that's where I set up. The proximity of doughnuts had nothing to do with it.

Disconnecting the microphone from its housing on the camera, I placed it on one section of the rectangle and asked that it be passed from speaker to speaker as the reports progressed. It seemed a simple enough request, but as it turned out, it was anything but. Most often, as they began their speeches, the department heads were concentrated on what they had to say and simply forgot about the microphone. Whole speeches were made out of range of the mike, or, if audible, were often wiped out by the sounds of paper crumpling or low-voiced comments from people near the forgotten microphone. When they did remember to pick it up and use it, the microphone often became a form of emphasis as speakers gestured dramatically, effectively bouncing their voices in and out with each sweep of the arm.

Even if the conference had not been scheduled to last about 8 hours, it would have been impossible to keep the camera absolutely still for any appreciable length of time without a tripod. But using a tripod created its own set of problems. Holding the camera stationary locked me into a single spot for each segment, regardless of where the speaker might be located. I could tell from the agenda which person was scheduled to give a report, and I could set up accordingly; but in the discussion that followed, anyone, from any point on the compass, might jump in and talk. This often led to the effect of a disembodied voice emerging from a cluster of heads turned away from the camera's point of view. Not only was this bad video, but it effectively destroyed any benefit that the speaker's expression might add to the presentation.

One corollary rule I learned that day was: don't assume that you must be the fly on the wall and never intrude on the proceedings. Without being a total boor, you must be ready to explain, in simple language, exactly what you need people to do in order to make a tape work in their best interests. And be firm when you do so.

I found that I could not move the camera without literally lifting the whole assembly and carrying it. If I did it while the camera was still running (don't forget, at this point, I was scared to death to turn it off!) this did interesting things to the tape, showing dizzying sweeps of the walls and ceiling. Needless to say, I did as little moving around as I could get away with while still taping the person doing the current report.

The major advantage of using the tripod, as I said, was that it kept the camera steady and yet gave an impression of movement through panning the crowd or zooming in and out on each speaker — at least, on those speakers within my camera's reach. In the excitement of the moment, however, I forgot about the effects of swift in-and-out zooms and fast pans. Between my moving the tripod and those cavalier zooms, it takes a good dose of Dramamine to make parts of that tape watchable.

Another aspect of my learning experience was that I discovered what happens in a lighting situation when half of the target area is in bright natural sunlight flowing through windows, while the other half is lit by fluorescent overhead lights. One of the major differences between still photography, something I was familiar with, and video — something I only thought I knew about — was that you have to deal with swift changes of light that are all part of the whole scene. There are no separate shots for which you set your camera and just leave it until you're ready to make the next shot.

What I got were startling color changes as the camera moved back and forth, the likes of which could have provided special effects for any number of horror films. Warmed by sunlight, faces faded from off-yellow to rainbow-rimmed white, their features dissolving in the glare. In fluorescent light, green tinges and distorted shadows gave them a sickly, other-world aspect. By moving the camera in a slow pan, I was able to swing through the full spectrum of bad lighting and create monsters out of perfectly amiable people. We won't even go into what happened to white shirts or patterned jackets.

I wasn't familiar enough with the built-in camera filters to offset some of the problems I encountered. As a matter of fact, even checking my shots on the monitor didn't give me the full effect. It was only later when I reviewed the tape in its full glory that I discovered all these flaws.

This variety of visual and sound problems would have made these eight hours of recordings usable only if our target audience happened to be the general public on the "World's Funniest Videos" and not library staff and trustees. The whole idea of taping was so new, however, that we were thrilled that we had done it at all. Each of the department head/speakers came to the editing suite later to check their own segments, and as you might expect, they were more concerned with how their hair looked and how their voices sounded than they were in criticizing the technical aspects of the tape.

THE DAWN OF POSSIBILITIES

Live and learn. If you look at the "videography" at the end of this book you'll discover several early tapes that sound more like home movies than polished productions. That's because they were.

Part of the problem at the beginning was the fact that our administration and board had no real concept of how the medium should be used; they felt many situations merited review, and taping meetings and conferences would provide an easy method to refresh their memories. It was unrealistic on their part, though, to believe they'd really want to watch hours of tape to clarify one or two points. Because of this, many productions we made as a "record" often languished on the shelf. But it's almost axiomatic that a library would be interested in keeping materials as records, without thinking in terms of quality or usefulness. At that time, we had no role models to learn from, and everyone in the library thought they were experts on television — after all, didn't they watch it all the time?

Nobody had any concept of how big cable television was going to get, though. Because of that, our city's long-term cable contract didn't include a provision for public access, something that was automatically built into later cable contracts by other communities. Those contracts often included funding from cable revenues to help provide the public with access to local programming facilities, and in some places that money went to local libraries to create seats of public access.

Despite the fact that we had no recourse to cable revenue, I had been looking for some way to use our local cable company to help us air original library productions. I discovered that there were two "unused" cable channels available for public access, if the city could provide a minimum number of hours of programming each week. It was obvious that the library couldn't fill all those hours, but in conjunction with the Police Department, the Fire Department and the Health and Social Services Departments, we might be able to create enough programming to do the job.

The Board was enthusiastic about the concept and asked me to write up a proposal for thirteen weekly magazine-style programs. We also made up a schedule of story hours and library orientations that could be shown live or on tape to help fill the library's share of programming. I had no problem coming up with ideas that filled the bill. Our first program would be about children and the arts, as an example of how library offerings tie in with other cultural entities, especially with an emphasis on young people. Other subjects would include how the library's resources could help in formulating an intelligent job search, as well as detailing the histories of major corporations and businesses in the area.

We had even received encouragement from a local news organization willing to sponsor and promote our programming. Other city agencies expressed interest in the concept as well, but it was impossible to get them together at one time to describe the full advantages of such a cable outlet. Explaining it to one group at a time proved to be pointless. As often happens in such cases, the availability of those channels disappeared when cable demand increased, and access to them was lost.

There were internal changes in the library about that time, due to sharp cuts in funding from the federal level on down, so except for some off-air taping and film chain work, we shifted attention from production of original works to promotion of our rapidly growing collection of commercially produced videotapes.

For those of you who are not familiar with the terms *off-air* or *film chain* taping, let me briefly explain. Off-air taping sounds glamorous, but it's exactly what you do when you set up your home VCR to tape a program. The difference here is that when a library does that, it's to add the program to their collection for patron use. The law requires that when such taping is done, permission has to be sought and licensing purchased.

At the time we were doing it, such licensing was extremely expensive; it was only through a state grant through the Racine County Library System that we were able to do it at all. Once paid for, though, the taping itself was relatively easy. And to emphasize the fact that we had done the taping lawfully, we designed a logo on tape displayed at the end of each tape to identify it as library property.

This process involved a simple point-&-shoot technique. We had no character generator at the time, so we literally typed up the information, added a graphic, taped it to the wall, and shot it with the video camera. And, of course, that's just what it looked like.

The film chain was something else again. The System had put aside a certain amount of funding to add particular items to our video collection to benefit the most neglected part of the video audience in the early 1980's, children. Not much was commercially available for them, and existing materials were very expensive. Most libraries in our area already had excellent collections of 16mm films geared to children's interests, however, and putting those films on videotape would make them available to home audiences as well as the larger audiences 16mm films were designed to serve.

Because the System belonged to a consortium of libraries throughout Wisconsin, we were able to access all of the films in their collections for possible conversion to videotape. After checking the titles owned, a team of professional librarians gave me a list of the films they wanted to have converted.

Two steps were involved in transferring 16mm films to video. The first was to get permission and pay for a license to copy the material. This was, as I said earlier, an expensive proposition.

Secondly, equipment had to be purchased that would synchronize the frames of film to match the speed at which video is shown on a screen. Without that synchronization, an irritating series of lines would run throughout the picture.

There's a long, fascinating story behind the number of lines on a television screen and the number of frames of a film that run past our eyes in a given period of time to provide an illusion of continuous action, but that story belongs in a much more technical book. It's sufficient to say that 16mm films and television screens do not travel at the same speed; but a piece of equipment, known as a film chain, can make them compatible.

A 16mm projector is lined up on one side of the chain, which projects the film to be copied onto a set of mirrors — the multiplex unit — deflecting the image to the video camera. The projector and camera are mounted at right angles to each other, each facing the mirrors.

When it works perfectly, little of the sharpness of the original is lost, and taping takes as long as the film runs. When it works less than ideally, the technician can learn just how expressive his or her vocabulary really is.

Films break, bulbs go out, the projector gets the jitters — a lot of things can, and do, go wrong. Clarity and color on tape often were inferior to the original film quality. It was not the ideal way to add material to our collection. But considering the circumstances under which we were working, it was the most practical way to get what we wanted, which was a broader range of children's films on video in the libraries.

GEARING UP FOR SERIOUS PRODUCTION

It was about that time that a different position opened up for me in the library and it shifted my perspective on video production. As the new head of the Publications Department, I had more latitude to use my skills in writing and graphic arts while I still retained my involvement in original productions. As it turned out, this period marked the start of our most ambitious work, because it gave the library a complement of two people who worked on ideas and their implementation.

We hired a full time video technician and began plans for what would soon be our own editing facility. The technician, Barry Johnson, sat down with me and together we brainstormed a number of possible productions that we believed to be feasible and exciting.

We presented these concepts to the City Librarian, and he was open to our plans enough to carry them, along with his enthusiasm for them, to the Board. The Board in turn gave us the go-ahead to spend time and energies establishing a video production element in the AV department.

Our first priority was to raise enough money outside the regular budget process to provide ourselves with adequate equipment for filming and editing. W ith the Board's encouragement, and a lot of help from the community, we were able to do just that. I'll go into more detail about the how-to of funding later on in this book, but for now, let's concentrate on how we discovered our audience and learned to meet its needs.

Since you've read about the experiences of our first production, it might be instructive to contrast them with the last one that I worked on before leaving the library. This production was one that truly fit the concept of meeting our audience's needs. It was titled, *Great Expectations: the Story of Racine on the Lake*, a documentary showing the complex process involved in a turn-around project that changed not only the face of Racine, but the way the city perceived itself as well. It went far beyond the simple business of turning on the camera and recording what was happening.

While our first video effort was strictly a matter of recording internal library activities and concepts, the "Racine on the Lake" project was a sophisticated piece of work based on events that affected the entire city. It was also something of a gamble, since the project we planned to record took a long time to come to fruition and faced a great deal of controversy in the process. We could easily have been criticized for wasting time and energy on something that turned out to be a red herring; but it didn't, and so Barry and I came out looking like very smart people indeed.

This last is not intended to show you how psychic we were, but to underline the fact that sometimes you have to take chances in order to get the job done. It really helps when administrators back you and allow you the opportunity to fall on your face from time to time.

The Racine on the Lake project was originated by a concerned group of businessmen who took their ideas and concerns before local government. But they went a step further than simply expressing their unhappiness with the crumbling status quo. They had devised a plan to focus attention on a critical area of our city's downtown, including an adjoining strip of lakefront property.

Less than two blocks east of the business district on Main Street, local fishermen enjoyed catching perch and other small game fish from concrete piers while others used a small boat launch to go after the bigger game waiting in Lake Michigan waters. It had great recreational potential, but it was a sleeping giant.

The giant needed to be wakened, and soon. In 1981 Racine was suffering from the effects of the recession devastating many cities in the Rust Belt, with local unemployment reaching as high as 16%. Businesses were closing, merchants were fleeting the downtown area, and a seedy, ghost-town aspect had settled like a pall on the city. In its March 2, 1981, issue, *Time* magazine referred to *"Racine, Wis., a typically declining industrial city. Razed or boarded-up buildings give its downtown the look of a community under siege..."*

It was grim, and getting worse. But there was a determination at the heart of the city to fight back, to come back up off its knees. What was needed was a rallying point, a showpiece to give new life and hope to the community. To accomplish this, Racine did something that had never been tried before.

Those first tentative plans translated into a coalition of city and county governments who met with those first representatives of private enterprise to attempt a miracle. It turned out to be an achievable one. The result of this unique coalition was a breathtaking new lakefront bursting with possibilities, complemented by a slicked-up, renovated downtown business district. In the July/August 1989 issue of *Wisconsin Trails* magazine, Tom Davis wrote, *"Comparisons to Lazarus and the Phoenix are probably inevitable, but if the renaissance of Racine is part miracle, it is no myth. Far from requiring last rites, the city is now robustly alive."*

The project began by relocating a car dealership and removing gas storage tanks, rubble piers and trash from the shoreline; in their place would be built a magnificent park/marina complex to attract boaters from surrounding states, notably Illinois, Michigan and Minnesota, and provide a new focus for expansion. Both city and county governments took responsibility for parts of the project, while private enterprise provided the boost and even some of the funding.

There was a flurry of controversy over these efforts; in every town, there is that small cadre of grumps who insist that "we tried that in 1937 and it didn't work," and this project was not exempt from their grousing. But to counter the critics who called it a rich man's toy, the new marina/festival park was marketed as a source of pride for everyone in the city. A particularly successful aspect of the selling of the project was the opportunity for anyone to "own a piece of the park." Everyday people began to donate money for the benches, wastebaskets (sometimes in their bosses' names), lampposts or other furnishings, which created a strong sense of ownership and pride in the park. One especially successful promotion called for a corner of the park to be paved with bricks, each engraved with a donor's name. A striking monument was later added to the brick-paved area to make it picture perfect. People can still be seen doing the "ostrich walk," head downward, poking along, looking for their brick.

NOT RAIN NOR SLEET NOR OTHER STUFF, EITHER

Taping the project covered a period of almost two years, from the time land was first cleared to the completion of the largest basic elements of the plan. In rain, sleet, sunshine or fog, Barry went out to shoot video footage of the construction as it progressed. Some of that footage was certainly dramatic, while some of it was pedestrian, but when we looked back on it during editing, it was all priceless in terms of telling a unique story.

From a visual viewpoint it was relatively easy to show construction progress on videotape. It required only a few minutes of shooting each week, or every couple of weeks, as visible changes took place.

Especially cinematic were scenes of huge trucks laden with stone and concrete as they rolled through the city and out onto the berm, which was a strip of land they created even as they used it. Sometimes we would watch them with trepidation, certain that these trucks would misjudge their footing and nosedive into the lake, but miraculously, none ever did. Massive chunks of rock and concrete were dumped progressively further into the lake and then topped with finer fill until at last concrete could be poured for the road, parking lots blacktopped, and a unique docking complex laid.

At the same time, sand that had been dredged from the lake to create sufficient depth for the marina was used as a foundation for sixteen acres of landfill that became a County Park and the site for restaurants, shops and a water patrol headquarters to serve the marina. Graceful buildings grew from skeletal frames to multi-hued completion, and the marina very quickly filled with boats, lending a bright, celebrational aspect to the waterfront.

Downtown had gone from brown-bag bottles littering the street to the most beautiful lakefront on the Great Lakes. Boaters from all over, but particularly from Illinois, had been attracted by the beauty and the relative low cost. We had the showplace we needed. And the library had the whole thing on videotape.

Our raw footage could document the construction process very well , but it couldn't show the complex and important story behind the process. For that, we needed something more, and that became phase two of our production. We set up interviews with key players in the game, those whose decisions and risk-taking made it all possible. Among others, we taped two Mayors, two County Executives, a City Planner, a former member of the County Board, and the director of what was then called the Downtown Racine Development Corporation (DRDC), each of whom would tell a different part of the story. Each had a different vantage point, and each illuminated the others. It was from these interviews that we reconstructed the story behind the project, using footage of the construction to illustrate the interviews.

We also borrowed freely and shamelessly from anyone who could help us. One interviewee, the former County Board member, had personal taped footage of such events as the Governor making a boat tour of the area prior to signing needed legislation; planning meetings of the original team; and footage of other marina projects in the country that had been used for comparison purposes by the study groups. We also borrowed some fascinating tapes of tests made by a corporation involved in designing the seawalls and berms.

Some footage proved to be more than fascinating, however. In one remarkable piece of tape, we discovered that a local dignitary had managed to scratch his groin throughout the entire historic process. We reluctantly jettisoned the tape, but we took a long time to stop laughing.

From those tapes that were useable, however, and from our own tapes, we began to construct a beginning, a middle and an end to the story, so that the final production would be as complete as we could get it. One more thing was needed: continuity. In order to tie all the loose ends together, I wrote a script that filled in the gaps using a combination on-screen, voice-over narration. Jean Jacobsen of the County Board, a woman who was totally familiar with the project and camera-wise as well, agreed to play the part of the narrator and did an exceptional job.

IT HELPS TO HAVE FRIENDS — PUBLICITY, TOO

The word soon got out about what we were doing. A local newspaper featured a story about Barry, complete with front page photo. This, in turn, piqued curiosity about the project from influential people in the city and gave us a little more support to continue our taping.

We needed that support. Keep in mind that the taping took over two years, and other projects constantly claimed our time. We never tallied all the hours of footage used for the project, but it was considerable. Rarely did any interview take less than half an hour; and most took longer, especially if the person being interviewed needed time to get used to the camera in order to come across naturally during the interview. It didn't hurt at all to have important people interested in our progress and having them make that interest known.

One very positive aspect of this public interest was the help offered us by a local corporation with post-production facilities we could only dream about. They helped us with special effects such as graphics and titles, and they even provided us with extra footage of Racine, especially some aerial views of the harbor. I'd mention the name (and you would recognize it) but we promised that we would not do so.

I think you'll find that in any town, the biggest company is often the one with the biggest interest in the community, and it never hurts to ask for help if you need it. If you believe in your project, and can show how it will benefit the community, you can count on people to come across for you.

When editing was completed, Barry and I set up a premiere showing for everyone involved in the lakefront project. This included city and county executives; and, since we gave particular emphasis to the cooperation between public and private sectors, we included Downtown Redevelopment people and local businessmen in our invitations. The Festival Hall, featured prominently in the tape, seemed to be an appropriate setting for this premiere. We felt a real sense of accomplishment when the people most involved in the project told us afterward that they were pleasantly surprised by the professional quality of the tape and that they felt it was accurate and well done.

This sounds very smooth and easy, but of course in real life nothing ever is. Still, because this project was of interest to a lot of people, we managed to overcome our obstacles, one by one.

It was the most complex production we did, in terms of time, effort and number of people involved. It was also the most successful in terms of audience.

And that's the point. In the case of the harbor tape, we accomplished several things at once. We were adding a videotape to the library's collection of interest to historians, architects, students of government and everyday people; we provided city

and county executives with positive PR about the project; and we
gave the business community a beautifully done record of
accomplishment that they could, and did, show off to good effect
all over the country.

WHEN IN DOUBT, PUNT

In fact, the tape was a hit before it even existed! I mentioned
earlier that it helps to have important people interested in your
project. To show you how obliquely this interest can be caught
sometimes, consider the story of one of the City's department
heads who was going to a national convention and wanted to
make a presentation about the harbor project. He suddenly
discovered that nobody in the government, or anywhere else, for
that matter, had any sort of graphic material he could use to
illustrate his talk. When he learned we'd been taping the whole
thing, he immediately called and asked for a 10-minute copy of the
tape. Since there *was* no completed tape at that point, we weren't
sure how to comply. But Barry had long ago learned how to punt
in such situations. He scanned random bits of unedited
construction footage, dubbed ten minutes of it in chronological
order, and laid in stock music for background.

The department head was delighted and showed the tape with
pride. He especially liked the fact that he was able to narrate his
own version of how the Racine on the Lake project got started. But
what he didn't realize was that he didn't have *the* harbor tape, the
one that would tell the whole story from multiple perspectives.

We at the library did, though. No one else in the community
had done it; no one else had thought of doing it but us. As I
mentioned earlier, there had been a lot of pessimism about getting
all the complicated elements of the project to work, from basic
funding to the complex legislative changes needed along the way.
Only those directly involved believed that it would really happen,
and they were much too busy doing the job to document it. That
made our production incredibly valuable to everyone who had
worked to bring the project to life, and that included people in
every part of the community.

The tape also gave the library a high profile at a time when it
was seeking public approval for an expansion project. The
considerable interest expressed by those involved in the project was
mirrored by the general public, who were even more anxious to
understand what was happening on the lakefront in terms of how it

would affect their lives.   Making this tape a part of our collection
helped to show that the library was responsive to the needs of the
community. Everyone had access to that tape regardless of who
they were. Just as the harbor renovation was intended for the
enjoyment of everyone, so was the tape that told its story.

WHY ARE YOU TELLING ME ALL THIS?

I repeat my premise: before you begin any video project, think
about what you want to say, and who will want to hear it.   Like
the old joke about real estate, there are three things you must look
for in a videotape — audience, audience, and audience.   Each time
we began a production, we started with the basic premise of asking
ourselves who would be interested in this particular theme.
Some of our productions were intended to be basically
educational. For example, we made two different tapes on library
orientation, and we also produced two films in cooperation with
the Unified School District for use in their curriculum. We
designed and produced library promotional tapes for the
expansion project campaign. Those audiences were cut and dried.
But we also made tapes that included several possible audiences
outside of an academic setting, as, for example, the Black oral
histories or the interviews with Vietnamese refugees living in
Racine. While these tapes were shown to specialized audiences at
premieres, they have been used in classrooms, shown at service
agency meetings, and viewed at home by the general public
because they gave an in-depth view of elemental parts of the
community found nowhere else.
Let's look at each of these from the point of view of audience:
The orientation tapes covered a number of bases, as a matter of
fact, but the main purpose was to produce something that would
give library patrons a better understanding of library services. We
conceived the idea of a tape running less than 20 minutes to be
shown to individuals or groups to illustrate how the library works.
This tape was also intended to free the time of reference
professionals for more specific queries and patron assistance.
Obviously, what you tell a child about library services differs
from how you explain those services to an adult. In addition, we
assumed that patrons would want to know more about the services
they dealt directly with, such as information services, than they
would about more behind-the-scenes departments like technical
services.

Both children and adults alike can understand how books and other materials are processed for circulation, the basic task of technical service personnel. So to save taping time and energy, we devised a combination script. One version emphasized adult reference and circulation services, while a second tape placed the emphasis on children's services. The portion of the tape devoted to each of these discrete themes took half the time allocated for the total.

For the next ten minutes we showed the other departments, with a brief overview of their functions and how they related to serving patron needs. This segment was added to both adult and children's orientation tapes. Simply by adding this footage at the end of those separate versions, we created two different orientation tapes aimed at the two primary types of patrons served.

A VIDEO YEARBOOK

For a special tape project intended for use at a Trustee's function, we took some of the footage, including out-takes, from those orientation tapes and created a more personal look at the people behind the scenes. We tagged them with names and titles, using our character generator to add captions. The finished product, which ran for 10 minutes, described the functions of each department and showed everyone who worked in the library. It became a sort of electronic yearbook, long before schools discovered the format.

The staff was a bit edgy at being in the spotlight at first, but when they saw the finished product they were delighted. The Board was equally enthusiastic, since their opportunities to meet library staff members were understandably limited. This production presented staff members in their workplaces, showing the work they did and how it fit into the overall needs of our patrons. It met a need and it was welcome.

BACK TO SCHOOL

Tapes made in cooperation with the Unified School District confronted us with the need for a different approach than we'd been using; we were addressing their audience, not our own. In one instance, Unified had already put together a script and knew they would be using this particular tape for elementary school children. It was a behind the scenes view of Racine's unique Zoological

Gardens, and included interviews with the zoo director, the zoo veterinarian, and others who cared for the animals.

The on-camera host was a Unified District teacher. Taping went quickly, and editing was relatively simple. Footage of beautiful animals captured the children's attention and provided them with painless lessons. It was our custom to make copies of the tape available through the audio-visual (AV) desk for the general public as well. Even though the audience we anticipated and directed the work towards was composed of elementary school children, the story itself could be enjoyed by anyone.

The second tape we did for Unified was another story. This time there was no clear message; our librarians had met with school librarians to devise a tape that would guide children in middle and upper schools in doing research on homework assignments.

But the message was muddied by a sub-plot: we were also expected to educate teachers about the problems faced by librarians when dozens of children all show up and want the one book available on an assigned subject.

To add a note of excitement, the librarians had been planning this cooperative venture for some time before calling me in to let me know they wanted the tape done. As a matter of fact, they needed it completed within a month — was this a problem?

School was letting out, and in order to get everything taped before there were no students, librarians or teachers to film, we had to move fast. Since we had no script, no actors and no plan of action, this did give us pause.

But the one thing you learn to do in video production is to think on your feet. I came up with a script that seemed to cover all the bases. Then we asked for and received from a local high school the services of two young actors accustomed to quick study and role playing. We were pleasantly surprised by the teacher and school librarian who performed important roles in the tape who had no acting training, but who did their parts extremely well. Thanks to all of them, we were able to concentrate on getting the best shots and moving along to the next one instead of giving acting lessons.

I gave each person a copy of the script and asked them to memorize their lines as soon as possible. As it turned out, quick memorization came in handy, because we wound up with only two days to shoot everything we needed.

One day's shoot was spent at the school, to the delight of the rest of the students; we used them in the establishing shots at the beginning, and those kids were not only cooperative, but showed great promise as performers. One young woman had planned to cut class that day, she informed us, but came just to be in the video. She managed to perform in a number of impromptu scenes in front of the camera, not realizing that she'd lose them all in the editing.

The second day of taping was spent at our library, where our long-suffering staff had to play their parts well without the luxury of rehearsals. The student cast would be leaving on vacation the following day, and there could be no retakes.

It was the kind of shoot you do with one eye on the script and the other on the monitor. Like film people everywhere, we tended to group our shots according to location rather than following a script from beginning to end. Working in a rush like that, we'd sometimes look at each other in panic as we moved from one setup to the next. Did we get everything we needed? Even marking the script as we went along didn't assuage that feeling of frenetic fear.

In the end, we did find a couple of places where additional footage would have helped. But we did what everyone in that spot does when faced with the inevitable: we punted yet again. There is always some way to get what you need, or else you decide you really didn't need it after all. In either case, you concentrate on making the tape as coherent as possible, always keeping in mind who'll be viewing it. Did you answer the questions they would ask? Did you make each point clear, without beating it into the ground? And did you take the best approach, neither deadly dull nor flippant?

In the case of the research tape, we didn't have to wait long to get our answer. The teacher/librarian group that commissioned the tape held a special meeting when editing was done. While they watched the final product I paced the floor like an expectant father. Barry and I were more nervous than we'd ever been; we had seldom worked with such a tight schedule, and were still not quite sure if we'd met all the hidden agendas.

It was always our approach to use a light touch. In this case, we had used as much humor as we could to keep the children's interest high. But would it fly with school librarians? Would it fly with our own librarians?

As the closing credits ran, the audience burst into spontaneous applause. They poured out of the meeting room bursting with enthusiasm. I heard, over and over, how much the students would enjoy the tape, how much they would learn from it while still having a good time. Everyone's agenda must have been accommodated in the final product, since it was made part of the school district's curriculum; it would also be available to schools outside of Unified through our AV desk. We had managed to *show* as well as tell. And all it cost us was a little more grey hair; in Barry's case, not even that, since he's blond and it won't even show.

WHAT ARE A THOUSAND PICTURES WORTH?

When it comes to getting some messages across, one picture can indeed be worth a thousand words. Convincing the city fathers that the library was overcrowded and in need of expansion should have been an easy job; the facility had no room to spare when it was built in 1958, and thirty years of new materials and services, even with the most cold-blooded weeding programs, had burst that little building at the seams. To alleviate some of the crowding, the Technical Services Department was moved several blocks away to an annex where it overflowed into three large rooms. In addition, the AV department had doubled in size with the addition of videotapes and was transferred to rented quarters in a newly built office complex across the street from the main library. My own offices, which included a print shop, were also housed there.

Each of these "solutions" carried problems of their own, of course. It was impossible to come up with an ideal way to handle overcrowding without coming back again and again to the idea of expanding the building, or constructing an entirely new, much larger, facility.

We had pleaded our case with the City time and again, using every method of persuasion and information in the book, including slide presentations, meticulous documentation and offers of tours through the dangerously congested underbelly of the library. All in vain, however, as the city struggled with basic problems of an eroded tax base. We also faced the bland indifference often shown toward library problems. It's considered a cliche to compare something frivolous with being tantamount to "stealing a library book."

Purveyors of that cliche are painfully out of touch with reality, as anyone who's ever worked in a library (or paid for a lost book!) can tell you. Far from being funny, the theft of library books is pandemic, robbing taxpayers of the most valuable and needed books from the shelves with impunity. And the price of a library book, even before factoring in the cost of processing, has risen out of sight to the point where an average novel runs $20-$30 and a reference book is priced in the hundreds.

START WITH A LIST

Two things were needed to deal with this problem. The first
was an automated circulation system, which would provide access
to information about which books were in house and which were
out on loan to specific patrons. The second necessity was a security
system that would halt book thieves in their tracks and prevent
what had been clocked as the disappearance of 25% of the
collection in any given time period.

If the City laughed at thefts from the library collection, they
certainly didn't take the idea of overcrowding any more seriously.
Life and property were bottom-line considerations, not children's
programming or a quiet place to read.

So, essentially, there were three areas that the Library needed to
raise public consciousness about: one, the need for additional space
in the library itself; two, automation of circulation and cataloging
functions to speed up and sharpen the process of getting materials
into the hands of the public; and three, putting in a security system
to drastically cut down the number of materials that walked out
and never returned.

The written word hadn't done it. Budget campaigns hadn't
done it. None of our vigorous and well-thought-out appeals had
done it. But there were two new pieces in the game, and this time
they were in our hands.

TWO NEW WAYS TO GET THEIR ATTENTION

Our first advantage was the new public and governmental
interest in the lakefront area where the library had originally been
built. With construction of a multi-million-dollar marina and
festival park just two blocks away, the library found itself in a very
high profile location.

Secondly, creating a sophisticated videotaping facility under the
control of the library made it possible for us to cram into an 11-
minute promotional piece all the facts that we wanted to get across,
with all the immediacy and excitement that good video can
engender.

And that's just what we did. A local actress, Jill Jensen, agreed
to work for us at our usual fee — nothing — to take our viewers on
a videotaped tour of the library and its agencies, to illustrate
vividly how crowded conditions had become and to detail, with
customized charts and other visual materials, just how extreme the

problem had become. We needed to show the facts, but we also needed to use the evidence of our viewers' eyes to flesh out those facts.

DRAW THEM A PICTURE

I gathered the most visually impressive statistics and anecdotes we could find and turned them into a hard-sell script. This was no time to pussyfoot; we had to produce the equivalent of a television commercial strong enough and sharp enough to convince the toughest audience in the world — the people responsible for allocating the City's budget among its broad array of needs.

We took three days to shoot the tape with Jill, following our sales pitch to the letter. Jill walked through the interior of the library and quoted statistics with strong visual appeal: over three quarters of a million items were checked out each year using methods designed to work for circulation systems one third that size, and we showed that easily, with the little Gaylord charging machine jamming as patrons waited patiently for staff people to check stacks of materials out, one by one, *clank, clank, clank.* We filmed patrons crowded into tiny little study spaces, elbows bumping together, and we panned stacks where 250,000 volumes were jammed into shelves designed to hold half that many. And then we took our show on the road.

In the process of compiling our research, we discovered that there were five other libraries in Wisconsin with a population and funding base close enough to our own to produce a good comparison with our situation. Having Jill talk about them was fine, but we needed more; we needed to show our potential viewers exactly what other communities had done to provide themselves with not only adequate, but occasionally breathtaking library facilities.

We visited each of those libraries with a truck full of video and sound equipment. Our Librarian telephoned ahead and explained our project, and for the most part their staff people were delighted to give us the grand tour. Sometimes their patrons seemed a little bewildered, thinking we were local television news broadcasters, but when we explained our purpose it was not unusual for them to direct us to their own favorite feature. I especially remember one woman who seemed to be bursting with pride as she showed off "her" library. "Isn't it fantastic?" she grinned, throwing her arms wide with pleasure.

We taped broad expanses of low, wide-aisled stacks, open, airy reading areas, and particularly enjoyed recording such attractive features as the splendid atrium in Appleton. This atrium encompassed the broad front of a basic, rectangular building, giving two- and three-story high plantings room to grow and enfold the visitor. Even with that delightful perspective, I don't think we truly realized what a treasure it was until the moment when Barry tapped my shoulder and pointed to something far below, in a sheltered spot at the base of the atrium.

A PICTURE THAT SAID IT ALL

Her lap overflowing with children's books, a mother sat on a simple wooden bench cuddling the small child beside her. They were oblivious to everyone, certainly to us, sheltered in their private bower. The boy appeared to be about three or four years old, totally enraptured by the book his mother was reading to him as they sat close together.

If our plan had been to illustrate the real purpose of a library — to build a love of books and learning from the youngest age on — this picture alone would have done it. We took video footage and slides of this perfect scene to incorporate in our productions. But mostly we just watched this lovely pair because it made us feel very good about working for a library.

And so we returned from our travels to the other libraries with footage that served to flesh out our cold statistics. Among all the cities we visited, not one was as large as Racine, and not one library was less than twice the size of ours. And every one of those cities considered automated circulation and a security system to be essential, regardless of its size.

When people had a chance to review the numbers, they were impressed. But when they actually saw on tape what other communities enjoyed in terms of space, beauty and public pride in their libraries, it was a knockout punch. Added to the new interest in lakefront development, this consciousness of how far behind we had fallen stung the public and city government into action.

That was in 1984. Within a year, it was no longer a matter of getting to library needs *some day*, but of how soon expansion could begin. By 1985 the library had a security system, and the circulation desk was automated in 1989. And most importantly, in the spring of 1989 the first shovel of dirt was turned over for the expansion project.

This event, of course, was videotaped.

EXPLORING THE PAST THROUGH THE PRESENT

Making tapes to illustrate solutions for specific problem areas can definitely serve the purposes of any organization. But the tapes I enjoyed making the most and that were seen by the widest audiences had a different purpose in mind.

When we started out, one of our original goals had been to continue the library's collection of recorded oral history. We had, buried in dusty archives, a number of old reel-to-reel audiotapes made during interviews many years before, but having the capacity to videotape such interviews presented us with a whole new way to approach the subject.

Audiotapes left reviewers with frustrating questions: what did the person who was telling these stories look like? Was there a sense of fun in the words, or were they absolutely serious? So many aspects of a story were lost when the speaker's expression and personality could not be seen. So much could be added to the words if photos, letters, even landscapes could be filmed and used in context.

After considerable planning, we decided to create our first oral history on video as a special celebration of Black History month. I had prepared no script; with this type of production, the only way to go was to create an outline and design a series of pertinent questions to keep the interview perking along and on track. It was a tricky technique, and I had very little experience with it. Nevertheless, with all the courage of the ignorant, I set out to talk with a wide variety of people in our black community and create from these talks a meaningful program. To make the best use of research time, we assembled an informal panel of Black advisors to help us determine the approach for this tape.

This group provided us with a number of ideas about the people they considered to be representational of the community. We took the leads they suggested and approached several people, but we also kept our feelers out for other possibilities, other points of view. It was important to me that we deal with real people, not prominent athletes or politicians or clergymen. It was my opinion, shared by many of our informal consultants, that there was enough space devoted to those people in the news already. It seemed more important to find people who could strike a common chord with the average people who comprised our viewing audience, thus corresponding to the traditions of oral history even in a nontraditional medium.

MAKING CHOICES

In the end, we interviewed a married couple who had made
gospel music the center of their family life; we talked with a Black
Muslim teacher about his childhood as a sharecropper on a farm in
Georgia; we heard the life story of an educator who developed
minority studies in Racine and provoked interest in them right up
to the White House level; and we did a verbatim taping as two
street counselors rapped together frankly about drugs, crime and
gangs in the city.

It's more than a little intimidating to try to present another
culture with fairness and clarity. In order to determine how well
our choices had worked, I asked our Children's Librarian, a black
woman who knew the problems of the city intimately, to view the
freshly edited tape before we showed it outside the studio.

She sat through the entire 100 minutes, murmuring from time to
time or nodding her head. As it neared the end, I glanced across at
her and realized that tears were running down her face. While the
credits rolled, she turned to me and gave me a hug. "It was
perfect," she said. I was ready to show it to the public after that.

WHAT TO DO WHEN IT'S OUT OF YOUR HANDS

Sometimes, though, I wasn't the one writing the scripts or
handling the interviews. One such case involved making a
documentary which was much more structured than our usual
production.

Eleven years after the fall of Saigon, there began to be increasing
interest in dealing with the problems and sorrows of the
Vietnamese war, and I wanted to examine how it had affected our
own city. I felt that it was time to take a less emotionally driven
look at how things had been then and how our lives had changed
as a result of this conflict.

It also occurred to me that Vietnamese refugees themselves
might have had enough time to draw conclusions about their
experiences and be willing to share them with us. While the
Vietnamese population in our area was not large, they had shared
experiences totally different from those of refugees who settled in
other places, notably California. We wanted to discover what those
differences were, and, if possible, determine how they had
occurred. I wrote a grant proposal to the Wisconsin Humanities
Committee for money to hire a professional humanist/historian to

conduct interviews for us with members of the Vietnamese
community living in or near Racine.

The Humanities Committee was somewhat skeptical about
funding an oral history videotape. It was something that they had
little experience with, and that small experience had been anything
but positive. I finally persuaded them to give us $1,000 towards the
project by showing that they would be providing an honorarium
for one of the top humanists in the area. We hired Professor John
Neuenschwander, a Kenosha college professor who just happens to
be an expert on oral history, and who also cuts an impressive figure
on camera.

It was his intelligent approach that provided us with our
editing technique. After preliminary research, he decided to
conduct the interviews around three basic questions: first, what
was your life like before the war; secondly, what was it like for you
during the war; and finally, have you managed to adjust to life in
the United States?

By focusing on this segmentation, Barry and I were able to scan
the raw tapes and determine how to edit them into three parts, each
addressing one of the key questions. We began the program by
pulling out of each interview quotes that fit within a framework of
stories about life as it had been before the war started. Each of
these people shared deeply personal memories of everyday
routines and hopes for the future, and their experiences came
vividly alive in the telling.

The second part of the tape zeroed in on how the war disrupted
their lives, and the dangerous and frequently dehumanizing ways
in which they escaped from Viet Nam. In the third segment we
edited together descriptions of their exodus to the midwest and
what they went through in the process of acclimatizing to a vastly
different culture. In a final segment, we showed brief clips as our
speakers summarized their feelings about what they had been
through.

Getting these brave people to talk about their experiences on
tape was not easy, but we did our best to assure them that we
would not use a cheap or irreverent approach. John, our
interviewer, was also pleased when he saw the finished tape for the
first time. Talking to them, hearing about their struggles and
sufferings, he became quite concerned that the program treat the
Vietnamese fairly and with dignity and respect. In the end, he felt
we had done so.

In a segment devoted to an interview with the American host for a Vietnamese family, for example, we heard the story of how one Vietnamese family reacted to being in a frightening and confusing situation.

When they first arrived in Racine, all of them, mother, father, and several children, spent every night huddled together in a single bedroom with the lights on, fearful of what the dark hours might bring. It took their host family a lot of time and understanding to help them overcome their terror. Part of the problem, of course, was the language barrier, since they had few words in common and used mime to communicate. Language problems became graphically to life for us as this host described her reaction when a refugee lit up a cigarette next to a "Danger/Explosives" sign. It's not a concept that lent itself easily to non-verbal explanations.

SHOW AND TELL

Whenever possible, we tried to set up a public forum to introduce our tapes, first of all to let the general public know they existed, and secondly to be able to get an immediate response to what we'd accomplished. It was important to get feedback on our productions to know that we were not straying from the mark and were hitting an appropriate audience. You'll find in your own productions that feedback is a marvelous device to keep you going in the right direction. And it can be humbling if you're not.

In the case of the Vietnamese program, we held a premiere showing at the Golden Rondelle Theater in Racine, one of the S.C. Johnson Wax Company facilities. The theater had originally been built for the 1964 World's Fair and afterwards reassembled in Racine, where community-oriented films, lectures and other presentations are regularly shown at no charge to the public.

We sent out special invitations to a broad spectrum of people from the community and advertised the event to the general public. Library administration and staff people sat up front, enjoying the excitement of a "premiere," as did many of the participants and their families. City officials, keeping an eye on what the library was doing with city funds, also came to see the show.

It was pouring rain that night, but inside the Rondelle it was snug and elegant, its carpeted interior echoing the egg shape of the building and making us all feel intimately connected. Most of the 300 seats were taken, despite the weather. We had promised a "talk-back" between audience and tape participants after the showing, and it proved to be fun and interesting for everyone involved.

Later, when reporters had finished talking to everyone and most of the audience had gone, an alderman approached me. He had always been an outspoken critic of the library and was very bottom-line oriented. He took my hand in his and I saw an expression on his face I'd never seen before.

"I've looked through someone else's eyes tonight. For the first time in my life, I really understand what someone else has lived through. Don't ever stop doing what you're doing," he said. He gave my hand one more squeeze and walked away.

That's what it's all about. We'd reached our audience.

SO WHERE DO WE START?

Achieving what you set out to do can be a really exciting experience. But you can't accomplish anything without the right equipment to get the job done. It's a fact that a lot of new technology comes out yearly in the video field, and that makes things both simpler and harder. What you need is a "shopping list" of basic equipment before you go running off to the nearest video store to set up your production room.

It's not necessary to have all the wonders of modern technology in hand in order to produce worthwhile programming. Especially at the beginning, you won't want to get into something that's beyond your means, either technically or financially. Only after you've done a few "practice sessions" will you have enough experience under your belt to judge what works for you and which of the "bells and whistles" will enhance future productions enough to justify the expenditure.

In the next chapter, I will help you discover what the "basics" consist of, and what they will cost you as you set up your own production facilities and editing suite.

TWO

Equipment:

What You Need

To Do The Job

TO EACH HIS OWN

The fact that people are seeing more and more badly done videotape on television masquerading as programming doesn't mean that they don't recognize good production values when they see them. When you start out doing your own thing, you can't be distracted by the idea that others are getting away with less than professional results. You're thinking about the future, not ephemeral ratings.

For that reason you're going to want to think very carefully about what you use to do the best job possible. Whether you start out borrowing professional equipment or renting over the counter consumer cameras and recorders, sooner or later you'll need to buy your own equipment. Having a dependable camera, microphone and recorder of your own makes all the difference in terms of setting your own shooting schedule and getting the results you want; and when it comes to putting it all together, there's no substitute for your own on-site editing facilities.

Trade magazines like *Video Magazine* for professionals and consumer type periodicals like *Video Review* carry descriptive ads in addition to helpful, objective articles about new equipment every month. Some of it will be more technical in nature than nonprofessionals will appreciate. But often such information can help you spot a trend that could affect future buying decisions.

One example of such forecasting could be articles about Super VHS recording tape offering longer recording length, which makes it more economical to use for home videotaping of programs. But a longer tape is no advantage when you're searching for some particular footage while editing. You may want to think through these and other cost factors when deciding between half inch and three quarter inch recording and editing equipment.

BASIC DECISION #1

And deciding on which format you will use is a very basic and primary decision, since it affects just about everything you buy except for your camera and some peripherals. Consider this: when it comes time to put a product on your shelves, it must be in a format that works for the majority of your patrons. VHS is what most people use in their home VCRs. While there are still many BETA machines around, it is not a significant enough format to influence your buying decisions. These are essentially the two forms of tape that most people are familiar with, and many of them are not even aware that the size of the videotape — half inch— is significant. I'll have more to say about that a little further into this chapter.

In the meantime, the best sources of information to help you make your purchasing decision may well be the places you go to shop for your equipment. While the cheapest prices will usually be found in larger cities and outlet centers selling electronic equipment, you should check your local yellow pages to see who deals in video supplies in your neighborhood. While the original price may seem high in comparison to discount outlets, go a little further than price and find out what's included in the purchase. If there's not a store near you, check the yellow pages for the nearest dealer in your area.

It often happens that specialty stores can offer training in the various pieces of equipment and cameras as part of the deal. Also, if you are going to be buying a full complement of equipment from a single dealer, it's possible that you can cut a deal to save a lot on markup. Keep in mind, too, that you can usually count on a lower government price for schools and libraries which can save you considerable money even before you remind them that you're tax-exempt.

See if the seller provides on-site service for the equipment being sold. If you can avoid sending things back to the factory for repair and tuneup, you can count on having it back in use much faster. While there are some simple things your technician can do to keep your equipment in top performing condition, everything needs repair or tuneup sooner or later. When that time comes, you don't want to be without it any longer than you have to be. But check carefully before signing up for long term repair contracts. It's one of the ways that discount merchants make more money on the items they sell, and they are seldom designed to be in your best interests.

A local dealer can have other advantages, too. Once you get to know the service people, you can count on getting some candid advice about which brands and types of equipment to avoid, as well as what impact some of the new technology will have on your purchasing decisions. They will be very upfront about letting you know when there's a breakthrough coming along in the next year's models that could make a particular choice right now obsolete.

DEFINE *OBSOLETE*

Well, let me rephrase that. If you've followed the trade show news for any time (and they always make the front page with their new offerings in technology) you're aware that every year the word *obsolete* gets a good workout. Take it with a grain of salt.

For example, the high definition television sets introduced recently are truly a breakthrough, and eventually may very well make the set in your home obsolete. But this is not new technology; it's been around a long time, and it will probably follow the path that color television followed when it was first introduced. It would be folly to decide to do nothing until you can make all your tapes compatible with that technology.

In its current incarnation, high definition television (HDTV) doubles the total number of scan lines from the current 525 line NTSC system used in the United States and many other parts of the world to 1,050 lines and provides for a wider screen that looks more like a theater, less like a box. (NTSC, PAL, SECAM, etc. are different, noninterchangeable, television world standards for broadcasting)

The Japanese have developed a system that does all this, but it's incompatible with NTSC, so American technology is countering with a series of competing systems that will be compatible;

General Instrument and MIT tested their digital HDTV system in December of 1991, and their second entry in fall, 1992; Zenith and AT&T completed testing theirs in May, 1992; the Sarnoff/Phillips consortium completed their tests in August, 1992; and in 1993 the FCC's advanced television advisory committee plans to recommend a winning system early in the year, followed by field tests. If all goes well, by the end of 1993 there should be an HDTV standard in place through the FCC.

If you check current ads for VCRs and television sets, you'll find that there are models available right now that offer 700 lines of resolution or more to American consumers. Odds are that one of the prototypes now being offered may win out over the Japanese version since it will allow implementation without making the estimated 160 million NTSC sets currently in use in our country obsolete. In the meantime, you might want to consider purchasing equipment that has this capacity so that your work will be the best, technically, that it can be.

HOW DOES THIS AFFECT ME?

All of this is interesting, and holds much potential for improving the look, if not the content, of upcoming television programs, but it has little real impact on what a nonprofit institution chooses to do right now in terms of production. If you're working with equipment that doesn't reflect the very latest trends, it doesn't mean that you have to stop doing what you're doing, or that anything done in a lower resolution format is doomed to the dustbin. Remember that Matthew Brady didn't let the Civil War go by without recording it just because photography might have the capacity to one day come up with the Polaroid.

The same thing applies to 8mm video. That, too, was "revolutionary" and was going to make half inch tape a thing of the past. You'll notice that, while the tape has found a market, and cameras designed to use 8mm can be found on shelves right alongside standard equipment, it hasn't eliminated anything but bulk.

On the other hand, BETA half inch tape is rapidly becoming hard to find, and pre-recorded materials are scarce in that format. BETA and VHS ran a race in the early 80's, each moving forward with longer playing tapes until VHS surged ahead and cornered a good segment of the market.

Remember, I promised to tell you more about videotape formats in this chapter. Here is something else to keep in mind while making those pivotal decisions. The success of VHS had nothing to do with quality; if anything, BETA is technologically superior, with its shorter path to the screen. But in a market where the consumer calls the shots, a longer-playing tape that looked okay when played back sold better than a shorter-playing tape that looked marginally better. Even so, BETA tapes can still be found despite industry predictions for years that the format was doomed.

One more revolution is here for consumers; BASF, the maker of high-quality videotape, has announced the development of a new tape equal to that developed in Europe, capable of recording up to 10 hours on a single cassette in the extended play mode. A company in Finland reportedly is working on hardware that will run at one-third normal speed, which could make a T120 tape run for up to 18 hours. If you combined both that hardware and the new length tape, you might never buy tape again, with a potential 30 hours of taping on a single cassette! But remember, if you don't keep track of what's on that long, long tape, you could get very frustrated trying to find something.

Keep these things in mind when you begin your search for the format and equipment that will work for you. Eventually, when you have your facility set up and a little experience under your belt, you may choose to select additional equipment from outlets or catalogs. You'll be in a position to be more aware of the downside of those purchases.

I HAVE A LITTLE LIST

Present technology is moving so quickly that if I were to provide lists of equipment by model number or other highly specific designation, it would be useless in a very short time. Think instead in terms of basic items that you'll want to start pricing as you set up your production plans.

When I speak of basics, I mean the very bottom line, those pieces of equipment that you simply can't do without. Right up there with the bread, eggs and laundry soap, this shopping list will remind you of what you need to start out right.

Your "shopping list" for basic taping:

- camera/batteries
- tripod
- portable recorder/batteries
- microphones/batteries
- sound mixer
- portable lights

Keep in mind that professional video cameras, the kind used by network news or even your local cable company, are probably out of your league. A studio camera alone would cost more than you will spend on recording and editing equipment put together. And you don't really have the need for anything quite that sophisticated, anyway. Consumer equipment has become so advanced in the past ten years that you can count on finding a superior product at a price much closer to what you can afford.

The consumer cameras that you'll be looking at can confuse you by the sheer number of available models and by the six different available formats: VHS, VHS-C, S-VHS, S-VHS-C, Super Beta and 8mm — and several new types will probably come out the week this book is published.

Each format has its own advantages, some of which we've already discussed; for example, the fact that standard VHS records up to 8 hours on a single T120 tape. The compact VHS-C format allows smaller camcorders to retain a kind of compatibility with VHS by using a cassette shell adapter. I use one myself to record family events, and I find that it's relatively easy to dub from the small cassettes in the camera onto the standard VHS deck if I wish to make a copy, with little loss of quality for that type of recording. Even rudimentary editing capacity is built in.

On the other hand, Super Beta camcorders have record only functions. 8mm is technically advanced, offering high-fidelity audio, compact design and more features. The S-VHS and S-VHS-C models have the best picture quality.

You can find such features as flying erase heads, digital effects, power zoom, variable shutter lenses and even improved audio and high resolution CCD image sensors to record alternate fields of the same image — but how often will you be handing out 3D glasses to your patrons along with your productions?

KEEP THIS IN MIND

Stick to the basics. Get the best camera you can afford. This is the time to learn an axiom that you'll live with forever: *you can't improve your tape once it's been shot.* The first generation is the best; everything after that gets fuzzier and fuzzier, even with the fantastic improvements that have been made in both tape and editing equipment.

Prices vary, but lower priced cameras come in at a bit more than $1,000, while the higher quality S-VHS models with digital effects and the kind of picture you're looking for start at about $2,000 and up. Count on paying between $3,500 to $5,000 for the camera that will give you the professional results you want with durability and ease of use.

There are two basic types of video cameras you'll probably be choosing between when you make your purchase. Three tube (RGB - for *red, green* and *blue*) cameras have three tubes, as the name implies. One big advantage of video cameras with tubes is the very good quality of video you can record, with high definition. Disadvantages include the fact that they are more easily damaged by bright lights and knocking about; they carry a higher price tag and are heavy to carry, especially with battery in place. And, they also need to be tweaked up from time to time to keep the image crisp and the colors balanced.

Incidentally, the word *tweaking* is a bit of technician slang for making adjustments to improve equipment function. If you try dropping it into the conversation to relax the people you'll be chatting with about equipment, you could look pretty silly. Remember, don't pretend that you talk techspeak, since that would put you at a real disadvantage with those who do. Let your pro speak to their pro when the time comes to do serious business.

To illustrate this, let me tell you about our first camera, which was purchased in 1981 and was not really up to professional standards; it was purchased by librarians and not video techs. I had no input when it was bought, but then, I wouldn't have known any more than the people who picked it out, anyway. We just didn't know the questions to ask. Hardly anyone did back then.

It served us well for about two years, and then the old style one tube technology began to fail; by 1984 the colors had been reduced to a dismal green tinge, and while our images were crisp when shown in black and white (achieved by turning down the color controls on the playback monitor), there was no way they could be used in real production anymore. All the tweaking in the world couldn't help. Today, however, while no electronic device will last forever, they are much less vulnerable than they were.

But let's get back to your shopping list, and let's hope your Tech is looking over your shoulder. The second type of video camera to check out is a CCD (charge-coupled device) or MOS (metal oxide semiconductor) solid state three-chip camera. These chips have replaced the tube image sensors, with negligible difference between the results of these diverse techologies. Among the advantages are lower cost for a high quality picture and a more rugged piece of equipment. Bright lights, for example, won't burn chips as they do tubes. Even equipped with battery pack, solid state cameras tend to be lightweight and much easier for beginners to use. Any banging around will also be forgiven more easily.

ONE TEST TO TRY

Check the white balance control on the camera you choose. This control adjusts the camera for different light sources, insuring accurate color. Some cameras have separate settings for indoor and outdoor lighting, some have automatic white balance, and some will have you set the balance manually. In our productions, we tried to remember to carry a sheet of white paper to check our white balance before every new shot, since ours was set manually.

Holding that paper out several feet in front of the camera, I'd wait for the ready signal from Barry so that we could begin taping. And for those times when we forgot the paper, we learned to search out other methods for setting the white balance, including having me turn my back to him in a white blouse, holding up a napkin from a fast food place (not recommended) or using the back of the script.

SONY and JVC make excellent brands of video cameras, but there are many good cameras from a variety of manufacturers coming out every day that shouldn't be overlooked. When we were making our pilot tape, a Kenosha hospital technician let us check out a Hitachi camera the hospital was considering for purchase. It was a fantastic piece of equipment, delivering crisp images in all light. Unfortunately, the popularity of that brand seemed to diminish while Panasonic's grew. You may have to sometimes choose the lesser brand, simply because you need to be able to get repairs and service in your own area or sacrifice the time to send it back to the manufacturer. It's still another one of those factors you need to consider.

The only way to be absolutely sure of a good purchase is to check out the better known brands, all of them, and make up your own mind. It's entirely possible that you can find the one camera in a batch that delivers far better images than others of the same brand. In this case, you don't have to be an expert to determine which is best in terms of image. Just check the tapes these cameras produce, and see for yourself what looks good.

Try taping something bright red, and watch for "noise" when you play it back. If you see grain instead of a crisp image, remember rule #1: it ain't gonna get any better.

Take your time deciding. Check with technicians at local hospitals, vocational schools, colleges, school district instructional materials centers and local businesses — wherever there are video facilities. See what their experiences have been, and if possible, handle their cameras to see how easy or difficult they are to carry and use. Check picture quality in every light. And be sure to allow for the effects of hard use on any cameras you might rent, since store technicians don't always keep rental cameras in top shape.

GETTING A FIRM FOUNDATION

Plan to add a tripod to hold your camera steady, but keep in mind that you'll want to be guided by your exact needs in this respect. Don't buy something so cheap that trying to use it drives you crazy; but don't buy something so expensive and specialized that you're frustrated by its complexity and wish you had something simpler. Get just what you need.

Here again, you will probably be given excellent advice by your local dealer. Buy the one that fits your camera. Look for the smoothness you desire when you move the camera. And think about using (and therefore transporting) that tripod for every shoot you go on.

Remember my adventures in taping the Trustees' meeting? While the tripod that I used kept me anchored in a single spot between setups, it also held that heavy camera steady for hours, enabling me to use zoom techniques to give an impression of movement to the tape. When we later purchased a tripod with a floating head, it made it even easier to handle the camera with smooth, gentle movements. If you anticipate moving the tripod around a great deal, you might want to look at wheeled units which can be added to some models. But that's a very specialized need and an expense that you may choose to do without.

Don't make the mistake of thinking that since you've seen people from networks carrying cameras on their shoulders, you can do the same thing. Those cameras are designed for that, the camerapeople are pros, and they don't tape for more than a few minutes at a time. Breathing and walking cause too much bounce, even with bracing units and other devices to steady them. Newspeople have their own methods of firming up the camera (unless they're trying for that trendy hand held effect) but nine times out of ten, when they can, even they will use a tripod.

When we first got our three quarter inch format equipment, I taped a department head meeting for practice with the camera on my right shoulder and the recorder on my left. In about ten minutes it became apparent that all 5' 2" of me was sinking slowly into the floor under their considerable weight. Each breath I took translated into monumental heaves on camera. Far from being able to carry it off, literally or figuratively, I found myself unable to continue, and slowly slunk back to my office, never to go on a shoot without my tripod again.

CHOOSING A RECORDER

Before you choose your portable recorder, you need to have made the big decision: half inch format or three quarters? Unless your budget is such that you can afford to buy both up front, you must choose now.

If you really had to, you could use a standard VCR for a recorder, but the problems with that are obvious. You have to carry and set up the VCR near a standard power outlet for your shoots, which makes the process far from mobile. It can work quite well for interviews, or almost any interior taping, but the minute you need to move from one place to another, you complicate things; you must eliminate any thought of exterior shots, for example, unless you can reach outdoor power sources. And VCRs don't travel well; they're not meant to, not even the lightweight new models. Only a portable recorder is really meant to be portable.

In choosing your format, keep in mind that the difference be-

tween tape sizes comes down to two factors: quality and cost.
Broadcast studios do their taping in the professional one inch size,
but many of them are moving to three quarter inch for cost savings
and flexibility. Most editing studios provide three quarter inch
computer editing for the same reasons (more about that as we get
into editing equipment). No one outside of the big studios would
consider anything but half or three quarter inch tape, since the costs
of tape and equipment for larger formats are so high that only the
most well financed stations use them routinely.

So we return to the question of half inch versus three quarters
inch. A quick rule of thumb says that the larger the tape, the crisper
the original image. In other words, a one inch tape will give a
crisper image than a three quarters inch tape, which will give a
better image than a half inch. . . but, and this is a big but, the difference between three quarter inch quality and half inch is diminish-
ing by the moment. You can get a really fine picture on half inch
tape, and when it's not been diluted by dubbing down multiple
generations, it can even produce broadcast quality results.

For those confused by the terminology, dubbing simply means
to copy a tape onto another tape. That second tape is a *dub* as well
as being a *second generation* tape. If you were to take that copy and
make a dub of it, the tape produced would be third generation.

If you have to copy tape that may already be a copy of the
original you should try to use a larger format, since beyond the
third generation most videotape images begin to resemble faintly
colored oatmeal

Another consideration will be the sources you expect to call on
to borrow tape footage. It may be that you'll need to have access to
a larger format recorder to bring the image onto your tape. See if
you can borrow rather than buy such a recorder, since they can be
pretty pricey. Some educational institutions still have their old U/
Matic machines, since it was the only format available a few years
back to play or record educational tapes. But most of those recorders were handicapped by being capable of recording on 20 minute
tapes only; the stationary three quarter inch machines can record
for one hour, maximum. Half inch tape can record for at least two
hours, and at long play, four to six hours on a 120 minute tape.
That's one reason why I hauled along a standard half inch VCR
table model instead of our three quarter inch portable for the day
long taping of our trustee's meeting. Imagine trying to capture
eight hours of discussion on 20 minute tapes.

HALF INCH USEFULNESS

Do I sound like I'm pushing the half inch format? I am, for several reasons. Half inch tape is readily available in a variety of lengths, though you may have to make your purchases through a supply house to get 30 minute high quality tapes, ideal for editing. If you find yourself out of tape in a strange town, you can count on finding VHS tape available in any store in town at minimal cost. Unless you've gone out of your way to purchase a knock-off brand — a bad imitation of the better known brands — it's unlikely that you will get a blank tape of poor quality.

Half inch recorders, true to type, will also be much less expensive to purchase than larger formats, and much lighter to carry. Prices are changing rapidly in this field, but you can probably expect to get an excellent portable VHS recorder for about $1,000 to $1,500, though you may find something even less expensive that works well. Shop carefully.

The portables come with rechargeable batteries and generally give you a good long run for your money — at least an hour on each battery, barring use in very cold or very hot weather which kills batteries quickly. The types of batteries vary, too, but in the long run, the more expensive nickel/cadmium battery is probably your best bet. This is something to discuss with sales clerks once you've chosen the recorder, since they can tell you which batteries will last longest and can be recharged repeatedly with good results. You'll need to purchase a battery charger compatible with your type of battery, but they are usually made to order and present no problems with availability. Often they are part of the package.

Another advantage is that if you decide on the half inch recorder you won't have to drop down one generation when editing is complete in order to make your tapes accessible to the general public. If you edited in three quarter inch tape, you'd have to make a copy of it in VHS for patrons to use. Every time you can avoid dubbing your master more than once, you insure a better, crisper image for the end user.

Just to beat it into the ground a little more, the difference in cost of half inch editing equipment versus three quarters is significant. Keep in mind, if you go with three quarter inch recording, you *must* have three quarter inch editing capacity; and then you'll still have to copy your larger tape onto the half-inch format for the reasons we just discussed. This means having to buy equipment to deal with both formats. However, you do have the option to dub from three quarter inch tape to half inch and then edit without losing much quality.

CAN YOU HEAR ME NOW?

All right. You've chosen your camera and recorder. Are you ready to go out and do your own version of *Citizen Kane*? Not quite.

At this point, you will want to look seriously at audio equipment to supplement your excellent videotaping capacity. The right microphones and an audio mixer can make the difference between just okay and *terrific* finished products. You'll be looking for equipment that can supplement the shotgun (multidirectional) mike that probably came with your camera.

Again, there are almost too many varieties to choose from. But consider what you will be doing with them, and think about cost. A good microphone is not cheap, but it will outlast a dozen cheap ones and give you excellent sound along the way.

One or two person on-camera spots are best handled with lavaliere mikes, which clip on to blouse necklines or jacket lapels. You've probably seen them in televised interview shows; they're half inch long tubular (or circular, if windscreens are mounted on them) microphones on clips. Jill Jensen, a local actress, can tell some funny stories about what happens to all the cabling attached to those microphones, since she has had them run under her clothes, up her back and tucked into other interesting spots in the process of making videos for us. This is when it's wise to have both men and women helping with productions, since many people are particular about who places the microphones, and where.

Radio controlled microphones are another option, but an incredibly expensive and complicated one. Since I never, ever, had that kind of budget to play with, I can't comment on how well they work. But they sure *look* good.

When you have more than one or two people on camera at a time, a shotgun mike works well, though placing it for maximum quality can be a challenge (see the story in chapter 1 about the taping of the Trustees' meeting for a prime example). Don't worry; you'll catch on quickly with a little practice.

A sound mixer is absolutely essential for operating more than one microphone at a time, especially lavaliere microphones. Cam-

eras generally come with a single microphone input built in, with
no way to monitor the sound level as you're recording. The sound
mixer solves both problems, giving you multiple inputs and also
gauges for sound levels on each microphone. You can use the
mixer to regulate levels of audio during editing, as well, and perform mixes and fades to enhance your video.

Using a mixer also allows you to patch in different elements
onto your tape such as music and voices from different sources,
giving you complete control over the sound levels. And it provides
you with excellent, crisp sound every time.

The price of sound mixers covers a broad range, from the simplest at about $200 to the more sophisticated models at $1,000 or so.

I would suggest that you add one more thing to your shopping
list at this point. A good set of earphones is useful to help monitor
sound in crucial situations. They can be lifesavers, especially on
those shoots when you run the sound directly into the recorder
without a mixer.

Be sure that when you buy your microphones and mixer you
buy all the necessary cables to connect your various pieces of
equipment together. Since cables are likely to be your least expensive essential equipment, get at least one spare, and a set of multiple connectors as well. It will pay off in less frustration and more
flexibility when you're out in the field. If you break a prong on a
plug, your equipment won't work, period. And a new connector is
not as easy to find as blank tape.

PUT SOME LIGHT ON THE SUBJECT

Once you've purchased all of the above equipment, start looking at light kits. Get the kind that is as portable as possible without
sacrificing versatility. Good light kits tend to be heavy, however,
so don't let the weight discourage you from getting the best you
can afford. To have good video with any camera, lights are an
essential element. Unless you're outside in bright light, any interview or closeup shooting must be lit for optimum results.

Most kits contain three lights, complete with stands, barndoors
and other extras that allow you to direct the light and to hold
diffusing scrims. You probably won't be getting too fancy in terms
of lighting effects and colored gels at first, but it helps to know that
you have that option when you want it.

Keep in mind that the bulbs used in these lights are very hot when in use, and can burn out unexpectedly, so always carry spares. Handle with care, and they will pay off handsomely for you. Prices vary widely but a good kit can be gotten for around $500 or less.

There are small professional light kits that resemble nothing so much as a small golf bag; these are easy to carry and can add the touch of balancing light you need for some situations. But if you plan to do real production work, you need the help of three light sources, to provide the classic key light, back light and fill light.

A key light is placed directly on the subject, illuminating one side and most of the front. A fill light is generally focused on the background and helps the subject to stand out from it. It's this light that gives you a great deal of versatility when using plain sets, since you can mount patterned scrims on this light, adding design and even color on to an otherwise boring background. The back light goes on the side of the subject not illuminated by the key light. It's not as strong as the key light, so as not to wash out the subject, but it adds a softness and three-dimensional effect that would be missing if only a key light was used. It also helps the subject to stand out from the background.

If you're not sure how to use these helpers, there are many good books available outlining photographic lighting techniques. When dealing with a formal set, the same rules that apply to portrait photography apply to video.

If you're using fewer lights, you should try to produce some reflection off camera to give the effect of back light. Keep in mind, though, that shadows are not always bad; they often add a desirable effect to an otherwise dull shot. Just be careful about how shadows fall on faces. We once used a large sheet of white posterboard to bounce light back at a subject, softening the harsh, one sided light we'd been stuck with up to that point.

It's just as easy to carry three lights as it is to carry large posterboards with you, however. Only an inadequate power source would justify trying alternatives, and that's something you try to determine when you do a site check (more on that in chapter 6). In brief, these lights draw a lot of power, so one of the things you must do is make sure you won't blow somebody's circuit breakers when you plug in and turn on the switches.

LET'S EDIT

All right. You've taken this terrific camera, steadied it with a firm, easy to use tripod, hooked up the portable recorder, placed your mikes, lit your subject, and taped a gangbusters of an interview. Now you want to add this footage to the background material you've already taped, maybe throw in some borrowed tape, do some insert editing and voiceovers, add titles to the beginning and make an impressive credits listing at the end. We know that cut and paste is not going to do it. You want to edit that tape. You need editing equipment.

Springing up all over the country in many larger communities, commercial editing suites can offer sophisticated special effects rivaling anything seen on television. Such suites can add, delete or change sound, move colors, make breathtaking flips or wipes and produce incredible effects with your video footage. These places also provide quick editing suites for computerized edits before moving into the higher priced suites, and that's where the dream of using such facilities stops for most of us.

I had the mixed pleasure of visiting one of these suites in Madison some time ago and spent the day in shock. The equipment was breathtaking; the effects wondrous; the price, totally out of reach for all but top professionals with top budgets.

One piece of equipment translated a video signal into a computerized image that could then be stretched, squashed, colorized, rolled over, and added to any piece of videotape you chose. The price tag (in 1984) was $175,000. For some reason, the Administrator wouldn't let me get it. But you can see its modern descendants at work whenever you watch a certain beverage commercial linking dead film personalities with modern pitchmen in seamless montage. It is tempting stuff, isn't it?

But enough of dreaming. As you go through the list of new technology compatible with the size of operation you will be contemplating, you're going to find many ways to achieve similar effects at a price that won't leave you in shock.

Let's assume that you'll be starting with a simple basic editing suite for your own use. Or you might be able to split the cost with another agency that's into video. But beware of partners who may take more than their fair share. Make sure there is an equitable arrangement for the use of editing time.

Because editing takes time. Figure a minimum of half an hour of edit time for each minute that winds up on the master tape. Far from being excessive, this is a very conservative estimate, since the best productions use techniques that take time to achieve. While some editors could conceivably get carried away with perfection (more on that in chapter 7), keep in mind that this is not something that can be done well in a rush.

TAKE THIS LIST TO THE MARKET

Here's your shopping list for editing:

- source vcr
- recorder
- control
- color monitors
- character generator
- special effects generator (optional)

Editing equipment — a source machine, recorder and control panel — are usually sold as a unit. It's not as complicated as it sounds. The source is a specialized VCR on which you'll place the raw tape that you'll be editing; the recorder is another specialized VCR that holds the blank tape destined to become your master tape. Both machines are controlled through a central panel which does much more than just move the electronic image from one tape to the other.

The editing controller will give you a digital readout from the tape machines to let you know exactly where you are in the editing process. The machines themselves read the electronic impulses as they run past the heads. The analogy to film might be to equate these pulses to the sprockets on film; the controller counts those frames, at your direction, and will play a scene from frame number 42 through frame number 85, and then stop. It will also allow an extra frame at each end of the scene to allow for the loss of a frame, or picture, in the process.

On larger tape the editing process can be much more complex, feeding tape from multiple sources; it also requires a more complex taping process to stabilize editing. Your technician will know how to handle these variables, so let's just go into a brief overview of what is done in the process of editing.

The simplest way to create a videotape production was described in the introduction, when a so-called educational film was made by turning on the camera, setting the focus, and letting the tape run while the professor standing in front of a blackboard droned on and on.

Had the cameraman taped other material and then added it to that same tape, it would have become a very simple assemble editing job. The only problem he'd face was the possibility of a glitch — a brief smear of color — where the two or more pieces were joined. Low budget, low ulcer editing, to be sure; but a total waste of the possibilities, showing complete insensitivity to the expectations of the viewer. A video production should always display a subject in the clearest, most interesting way possible.

Assemble editing, as you may have gathered from the above, consists simply of transferring large blocks of material from the source tape to the master. You probably do it at home, if you have a home video camera.

Insert editing, on the other hand, lets you choose an exact point of insert and exit for cover shots, interviews, or voice-overs, adding visual and audio effects together or separately at any point on the master. All these decisions are run through the control panel, which will let you preview your choices before making them irrevocable, thank heavens. That's the technique we used in creating a pilot tape, and that's the technique we used in our production facilities at the Library.

You've seen insert editing any time you've watched a program in which, as the person on camera speaks, the words are heard but the face disappears, replaced by pictures of what the speaker is describing. If those words overlap for a second or two into a subsequent scene, the audio has been edited to achieve that effect. It's a marvelous device for moving the action along, but it can also be a life-saver as well.

Barry once taped some interview footage in Janesville. When we reached home we discovered that we were missing a brief bit of footage to integrate that interview with portions taped at our own library.

Our intrepid technician pulled a rabbit out of the hat by taking a single word from the first tape and dubbing it onto the following footage. This immediately linked the two, and made it look as if the question asked and its reply were part of the same interview. In fact, they had been done many days, and miles, apart.

There's no denying the temptation to take portions of one statement and add it to portions of another, to take things out of context and make it appear that people are saying things they never said. In fact, you often see whimsical use made of this process in a variety of ways, not always benign. But since our purpose *is* a benign one, we can use it to make people look smoother than they were on the raw tape.

We'll get into that a little more in chapter 6. But I do want to warn you that intellectually understanding the ability to change things almost at will is not quite the same thing as actually sitting there in the editor's chair and doing it. Be careful that you don't get carried away with the process. Not everyone you deal with will have a well developed sense of humor.

I HAVE A LITTLE LIST

Let's talk more about your buying decisions at this point. No matter which format you choose, you will need to purchase two video monitors, one for viewing the source tape, and one for viewing the master tape. Obviously you need to be able to watch the process, and these two monitors make that possible. Small sets are preferable to large ones, both in terms of space and cost. But don't become penny wise and pound foolish by buying small television sets instead of professional quality monitors.

A monitor has a variety of connections for easy compatibility with your editing equipment and will feed information directly from the source and editor. What you see will be exactly what is there. When you're working on a tight edit, it can make all the difference in the world.

Keep in mind, too, that when you check out a purchase, many monitors are actually much less bright than consumer models. Look for snow, or grain, in the red areas. Blacks and whites should be very crisp, and the edges of the screen should be as bright and sharp as the center. A good test for a monitor is to run colorbars into it and check color and clarity. Prices can run from $200 to $2,000. You choose.

When it comes time to show off that finished product, if someone gives you more money than you ever anticipated you could look at projection systems to view your tapes. Or you could do what we did and borrow them. But for production, stick to the little monitors. Prices for projection televisions range from $2,000 on up, up, up.

Your editing equipment purchase depends on the choice you made when you bought your portable recorder. Did you choose half inch or three quarter inch tape? If you chose half inch, you can count on paying around $5,000 for a basic editing system: source, recorder and control. For $10,000 to $15,000 you can get an excellent VHS editing system, including monitors, CG, audio board and cables for hookup, and produce a great product.

Half inch production systems translate into a much lower system price, more portable equipment for different configurations and lower tape cost. They will produce an acceptable product for inhouse or public viewing. However, the downside is that half inch edited tapes are sometimes shaky if used for broadcast purposes. They can, however, be professionally dubbed up to a larger tape format and the quality cleaned up. The cost is high, but there might be an instance when it becomes worth it to you.

Improvements in half inch editing systems have been astonishing; when we used the equipment in Kenosha's IMC facilities to create our pilot program, the machines were subject to overheating and often refused to allow pinpoint insert edits without annoying glitches. When we purchased our own editing machines just a couple of years later, there was no such problem. Not only that, but the quality of each generation of tape has increased dramatically. It's obvious that these systems are getting better while the price stays reasonable.

Three quarter inch editing systems, on the other hand, will cost about $15,000 to $25,000 for the same setup: source, recorder and control. It translates into a large expense for a small improvement in quality over the half inch format. There are also more long term expenses; as mentioned before, larger sized tape is expensive and gives you considerably less recording time, with available tape cassettes running from 20 minutes to a maximum of one hour. One major advantage, however, is that you can use any special effects unit with larger systems.

NOW FOR SOMETHING REALLY SPECIAL

Panasonic makes a great special effects generator for around $3,000 that fits in well with a half inch system, so if you decide that this is something you really want you're not bound to purchase those wildly expensive models in order to have it. Character generators and special effect generators are the bells and whistles of your editing suite. For most purposes, you will want to use a CG instead of any text production abilities your camera may have built in. Parenthetically, you would only want to impose date or time information directly on tape that's intended to be used for legal or law enforcement purposes. It's impossible to remove that text from footage if you want to use it in your productions.

Get the best character generator you can afford, but at the very least, make sure that it will provide you with colored text as well as white. More fonts and font sizes are bonuses. The price tag is not cheap; CGs begin at about $800 and go up into the stratosphere. If you are feeling really flush, you might want to get a combination CG and special effects generator.

Special effects can include such elements as the basic types of digital art: the mosaic, a system breaking the picture into hundreds of tiny squares; and solarization, which exaggerates colors to add an artistic effect. It's basically the same technology that I anguished over in Madison, but on a far less expensive scale.

The technology in Madison also allowed for digital superimposition, which means taking a computerized image and superimposing it on videotape (like the cola ads). It's become a common feature on special effects boxes and is even available as part of the built-in features of some commercial camcorders. Special effects generators will allow you to perform such wonders as wipes, fades, digital effects, video switching with a variety of inputs and outputs, and even some built in audio mixing.

COMPUTER CAPERS

A possible alternative or addition to this would be the use of a computer to interface with your video. One source of information about such interfaces for those using the Apple brand of computer is an annual Macintosh buyer's guide, which sells for about $5.00. It lists hardware, software and peripheral accessories that deliver the effects you're looking for. Cards can be mounted in older Macs; a digital film recorder will work with newer models, as will boards such as ColorBoards; the Cromatron is a video scan converter with standard NTSC video output for the 512 or larger Macintosh; and there is a Genlock Converter that works with Macintosh II models and up through a video interface card to perform special effects directly on the VCR or video projector. These are just the tip of the iceberg, but keep in mind that it's an expensive iceberg.

For those who prefer the IBM format, my son the computer expert tells me that San Diego City College, where he runs the computer labs, produces educational videotapes using IBM software for their special effects. Amiga computers, as well, are tops in graphics and animation and are compatible with the IBM. Look around, and you'll find still more brands coming out with this capacity. Schools and libraries are already geared into computers, so it might be worth your while to look into the prospect of using them for video special effects and programming.

Some caveats: the newer formats we spoke of a while back, such as S-VHS, are analog, while computers are digital. Each video frame must be digitized, and this can compromise the quality of output.

Computer video output and standard television run at different speeds, use different arrangements of signals and form pictures out of different numbers of lines. Make sure you know exactly what you're getting into before deciding on this course.

Since we didn't have the use of either a computer or a special effects machine when we were doing our tapings, I can only tell you that they would have been wondrous things to have. We were able to borrow special effects for our production titles from a local corporation, but we didn't want to overdo it, so our requests were few and far between.

I have used computer software that translates images from videotape to computer, but it requires a lot of ROM, not to mention RAM, to create a decent copy for your printouts. It's not the most practical use to make of your tapes, unless you do a lot of PR work in conjunction with your productions.

Beyond what we've discussed lie the proverbial *black boxes*, those pieces of equipment that add special features to your productions. There are synchronizers that work with time base correctors to give synchronous A/B roll editing, but they could cost you as much as your whole editing system; professional editing consoles that do such synchronous work cost upwards of $20,000, however, so price is relative. Editing and dubbing equipment exists that will give you remote control over video stabilizing, color enhancers and correctors, and software enhancement. Prices on these goodies range from as little as $50 to $2,500. Let your technician choose among the bounty of video processors/enhancers/stabilizers that will improve color, crispness, and sound while not emptying the pocketbook.

When we first started setting up our production room, we put
the equipment we used on large library tables and later added a
couple of AV carts to hold monitors and VCRs for replay. These
proved valuable for setting up showings when there were more
than a few people in the audience. But as we got into more elaborate work, the Friends of the Library group purchased an authentic
editing desk for us, which housed the monitors at a perfect level,
put the control panel neatly in front of the editor, and housed
peripheral equipment close at hand. The ideal setup is similar to
that used for computers, so that the person operating the equipment can reach everything from the chair. This saves a lot of fatigue, and contributes to the fact that editors are always on diets.
Barry adds this footnote: a comfortable chair is an absolute necessity for those twelve hour stints at the board. Amen.

Having an AV cart close at hand made it possible for Barry to
hook the character generator up and use it through a large monitor,
leaving the two smaller monitors to service the editing process. We
were also fortunate enough to have a sound setup that incorporated stereo playback equipment and let us transfer recorded sound
and music directly onto the soundtrack of our tape. Putting sound
on videotape makes it easier to control with pinpoint accuracy,
adding it in at whatever level is desired, raising and lowering it to
suit your needs, and cutting abruptly or fading.

But we didn't purchase that stereo equipment; it had been part
of the library's unused AV equipment. We were delighted to give it
a more purposeful life in the editing suite. Before we got it, though,
we were able to use a standard tape recorder to feed sound onto
our videotape, so if you don't happen to have spare stereos around,
a relatively inexpensive tape player will fill the bill nicely.

In Kenosha, the large number of VCRs and monitors used in
their Instructional Materials Center made it efficient for them to use
a switcher to interface equipment pieces at random with a cable
switching device. Such switchers are relatively simple to use and
save a great deal of cable moving. You may want to consider this
as a possibility when you set up your gear. Switchers tend to be
inexpensive, depending on the complexity of your setup.

MAKE SOME NEW FRIENDS

Again, check current periodicals for more information about
what's new out there, since the technology advances hourly. One of

your best sources for information is your fellow video producers, so keep your lines out to all those in your area who are in any way involved in video.

When the library first started production, we put out just such feelers to educational and corporate producers and soon found ourselves in a video users group, one that proved useful in a thousand ways. This was hardly a unique desire of our own; everyone in the Racine, Kenosha and Milwaukee area who was into video was blazing new ground and wanted desperately to have someone else's experiences to help them along.

The most aggressive video users in the area seemed to be in Kenosha, and they formed a producers group called SEWAVE - or South Eastern Wisconsin Audio Visual Educators. We had teachers, librarians, medical personnel, business trainers and many others in the public and private sectors who would meet once a month at each other's facilities and trade hands on advice, counseling and information on new technology.

Unfortunately, it was also about that time that many companies and non-profits in the area were cutting back on non-essentials, and video production, being so new and untested in the early 1980's, became one of the first casualties. The group disbanded and was never revived.

But it had been an excellent way to keep everyone in the field in contact, helping each other and learning new things. It's something you may want to consider starting up in your own area. While there are obvious differences in audience and needs between a library, say, and a hospital or manufacturer, there are also a lot more things that they have in common; and besides, it's wonderful to know where to borrow a spare floodlight bulb or cable if you find yourself in a pinch.

As a matter of fact, those same connections helped us many times later on when we needed information or the loan of additional equipment for two-camera shoots.

When you set off with your shopping lists, keep in mind that the best way to begin is by gathering information from just such places. Once you purchase your initial equipment, you can use these sources for help in all the other phases of production and editing, too. It's a good neighbor policy that pays off for everyone involved.

With user groups and a helpful local dealer, you can keep on top of every new technological advance as it becomes available.

While you won't be in the market for everything you learn about, you may be able to figure out a way to replicate some of the more interesting effects, on the cheap, of course.

And just how cheaply you want to operate depends a lot on the type of financing you can count on to fund initial purchases, as well as any upgrades you may be considering in the future. Upfront costs are the big ones, so it helps to know the size of your piggy-bank. Before you take the list you've compiled of what you need to get started to your Board — who may then have a collective stroke — move on to the next chapter and find out where else you can go to find the money.

THREE

Funding:

Where To Find The

Money

WHERE IS DADDY WARBUCKS WHEN YOU NEED HIM?

You've already figured out that there are ways to do things on the cheap; but there's no way to produce original video totally without cost, especially when we're talking about start up expenses. Nailing down sources to pay for these bottom lines is the next step in your move toward original video production.

As you've already learned, you need to plan on buying a good camera, portable recorder, and sound equipment. You'll also need the basics for editing. You'll stockpile a reasonable supply of tape. All the bells and whistles are wonderful and can enhance your productions.

Check over the list of what you need to get started. Once that's drawn up, you can start gathering prices to firm up your plan of action with definite startup costs. It's always a good idea to come up with a basic plan, a secondary plan, and a dream plan, and plug in the numbers for all three eventualities. Settle for the basics if you must, but have a wish list ready; you don't want to blow the opportunity to make the most of any unexpected windfalls by not knowing exactly what you will do with it.

One way to get what you need at minimal cost is to check the reference desk of the library or head for the city attorney's office to get yourself a copy of the contract between your city and the local cable company.

The cable contract in Racine, as I mentioned earlier, was not written to provide either equipment or funding for public access to cable television. But once cities caught on to the pot of gold cable companies have uncovered, more and more of them added contractual provisions to share that gold.

These days, in most of those contracts there will be a "public access" clause, often accompanied by specifics about funding and/or equipment usage. What you see in that contract will reflect the importance that the city placed on such matters; often the provision exists, but no one ever bothered to follow through and actually use the cable company's money or facilities.

In some towns the library was the facility chosen for building a cable-sponsored public access studio, complete with camera and output equipment for cable dissemination of programs. Libraries did not always greet this bonanza with cries of joy, since it was also up to them to staff the facility and help educate the public in its use. Library staffing has seldom been as lean as it was in the early 1980's, when such studios were being built. You can readily understand administrative reluctance to assign precious staff hours to something in which they had little real interest and over which they had no control.

Times have changed. Check that contract and see if you can have the use of cable company equipment, their professional assistance, or even a percentage of their net receipts to use for public video.

But be very careful here: you may still find yourself paying for these goodies with staff time and effort spent on helping the public to use these facilities. Not all users of this access are fine, upstanding citizens. You probably don't want your institution's name going out over the local version of *Naked Lunch*.

On the other hand, Saul Amdursky, who wrote the foreword to this book, tells me that he has worked out an excellent arrangement with the local cable company in which his AV people use that company's equipment to produce PR spots from library-originated scripts and then turn the raw tape over for post production editing by cable personnel. The agreement is equitable for both sides and provides the library with professional-quality publicity at minimum cost.

At the very least, however, cable companies owe libraries the same courtesy that radio stations and newspapers give them, to provide free PSMs (public service messages), which are preferably not aired exclusively at 3:00 a.m.

There is also such a thing as professional courtesy, meaning that the cable company should be willing to make copies of pertinent footage from their own files on your tape at no charge. Just keep your requests reasonable; asking for a copy of your City Librarian's speech from a local news program is okay. Asking that a network movie be taped for you is not.

The advantage of having the cable studio tape it for you instead of doing a straight off air tape yourself is one of production quality. Their original will make a fine, crisp copy. Your tape of the broadcast will lose a lot in the translation.

Having gone this route, you may find yourself in a situation where the cable people will grudgingly do PSMs, but no more; in that case, you must raise your sights and look elsewhere. And there are lots of elsewheres.

MORE THAN MONEY

Keep in mind, too, that funding isn't simply a matter of money. Help with productions, scripting and facilities can be worth its weight in gold. You can save a lot of time, for example, if an expert in a particular field is willing to do your research for you and provide you with written factual and anecdotal information. Local historical societies, preservation groups and professionals with a passionate interest in a subject are often willing to do the legwork for you, and all for free. All you would have to do is shape it into a useful script format.

The list of potential video angels is a long one. Most libraries, for example, have trust funds which can be tapped for nonoperating expenses. Developing new services for patrons might be considered by your Board as a legitimate use of those trust funds. But before you go after them, consider the alternatives.

Getting money from outside sources has two very important advantages. The first one is obvious: it conserves library funds for other uses. The second advantage is that donating money to the library's production facility provides the donor with a stake in the success of your video ventures. Mother, apple pie and the library are great selling points, but there's nothing like a credit line up there on the screen to pique interest in underwriting your projects.

In my own experience there are many local service organizations ready and able to supply funding, encouragement, and even PR to benefit both the work being done and the agencies financing it.

Ironically, the basis for our own video ventures was provided by someone who hadn't the slightest interest in the subject.

HOW TO SUCCEED WITHOUT EVEN TRYING

Our business manager received a phone call one day from an attorney's office. The City Librarian was out of town and the attorney needed a quick answer to a very important question: his client wished to remain anonymous, but wanted to give the library a gift of funds, providing the library could indicate — immediately — exactly what those funds would be used for. If the purpose met with the donor's approval, the money was ours.

Caught offguard, the manager suddenly remembered a recent department head meeting in which the hope had been expressed that the library could move beyond print and phonograph records into that new-fangled medium, video. It had been a wistful thought, one that was dropped because no one had the faintest idea how much it would cost to get into video in terms of materials and hardware.

Off the top of her head, the manager blurted out that the donation could be used to help the library open up a new type of service to patrons by starting a videotape collection. Apparently satisfied, the attorney indicated that the library would soon be seeing a check in the mail.

That check did indeed arrive, as proceeds of a stock sale by our donor, and it was quickly utilized when the library purchased its first commercially produced videotape titles as well as a camera, recorders, VCRs and cables.

Now, it's not likely that our anonymous donor will start running around the country like a fiduciary Johnny Appleseed dropping money wherever a need for video production is seen. But as you can tell from this story, being prepared to ask for what you want when the opportunity arises can only be good for you. Our donor may not show up on your doorstep, but other donors will, and it may be that their urge to buy $10,000 worth of chicken cookbooks for the library can be redirected into something a little more broadly based, like video production.

A good portion of our donor's money was spent creating a collection of established titles in video for our expanded AV office. It's hard to believe now, when you can buy or rent a videotape anywhere — grocery stores, convenience stores, hardware stores, even video stores — but when we first started looking for vendors, it was a tough search. Prices were high and deliveries slow. The video producers would wait until they had a sufficient number of back orders before they made copies of a title, and that could take a long time.

When the tapes arrived, we absolutely had to check them thoroughly before paying the invoice. It was not unheard of for tapes to be delivered with serious defects, including coming to an end ten minutes before the movie did.

This is no longer a common problem, and libraries can use machines to check tapes for flaws and dropouts which are similar to film-cleaning machines of the past. Still and all, these rather expensive devices can't tell you when a film is all there.

It's nice to know they still need people for *something*.

THE REST OF THE STORY

We had a little money left from our original donor, and after taping the pilot program and showing it to prospective funding sources, we were granted an additional two thousand dollars more from a local foundation. This money was squirreled away until we could raise enough to pay for editing equipment. As it happened, the wait lasted over two years.

A local Kiwanis Club finally came through for us, responding to our plea with a gift of more than $14,000. We added this to the previous seed money and were able to buy close to $20,000 worth of equipment including an updated camera and half-inch recorder.

A problem arose about what to do now that we had the equipment to create more sophisticated productions. We began getting rather strong suggestions that we should tape events of interest to our donors.

For example, a noted speaker was scheduled to talk to the Kiwanis; it was assumed that of course we would be sending our cameraman to tape the event and then give a copy of the tape to them. We did it reluctantly, but it required overtime for Barry and created a tape that was not necessarily of interest to the general public. At that point we realized that we had to set up guidelines. We could not become public servants of a private group. And we surely could not become everyone else's production house.

We finally decided to use the Kiwanis logo as an addendum to our credits, letting people know that they had made our productions possible. We also considered every request for taping using the criteria that it had to be an event of interest to the majority of citizens, which definitely narrowed the list.

Our Kiwanians were good sports about it, but they made it known that they wished us to concentrate on groups they favored with their charities: youth and senior citizens. We did make an honest attempt to focus on those two areas in our productions, especially since it fit within our own guidelines.

On the other hand, outside suggestions for subjects sometimes led us to worthwhile projects we might never have discovered on our own.

Two such productions were good examples of cooperative filming, as well. The first production, *Children Lost*, was requested by a local foster parent concerned with expanding public knowledge about the foster parent program. He had come up with a workable script as well as the cooperation of the social services department. His offer even included original music and a professionally trained director donating his services.

The director was a young producer with local roots whose experience in professional filmmaking proved to be the key to completing the tape in the two week period allotted for it. He had come home to visit relatives in Racine and was approached about doing the film by the foster parent, who was an old friend. He not only agreed to direct the project, but also prepared the script in cooperation with the foster parent and a social services representative. His abilities even extended to writing and performing two original songs for the production. But he had to leave town in two weeks to return to California, so that's where the tight deadline came in.

The script was intelligent and gave both sides of the foster parent story, including interviews with juvenile judges and local county executive, and showing alternatives to foster care. Since the foster parent had a background in community theatre work he was able to double as host and narrator of the film.

Our administrator okayed Barry's participation as long as it was confined to the two week period, involved no overtime, and left me free to handle other duties during that time.

I had mixed feelings about that, since I was dying to participate on some level; but the best I could do was wander past the editing room from time to time and peek in on the proceedings. On the other hand, permission would have been refused if my time was involved, so at least I felt I'd indirectly helped to bring it about. Some consolation.

One thing that had to be handled carefully was the depiction of children in foster homes because it would have violated the privacy of foster children to show them on videotape, even with their permission.

To make it all much more exciting for everyone, the weather turned incredibly hot. Our host found himself standing on the top of the 10 story building that housed the AV department trying to speak cooly and confidently while gusts of heated air threatened to make him one with the pavement. The broad background shown from the roof was intended to give an open, airy feel to the opening shot. And it really did look good on tape; his terror hardly showed.

The taping crew, actors and directors would all come into the library periodically, gasping and bolting down huge quantities of cold water, then run to check the raw tape and move on out into the hot sun again. Shooting was completed in the time allotted for it despite these hurdles. In two weeks it was ready to show to the library, the foster parents group, social services department, and representatives of the city and county government.

This was the first time I hadn't seen a production before we set up a premiere for it and I was especially nervous about the tension that seemed to have grown up between the foster parent group and the social services reps. Up until the successful showing of the tape, the foster parent organization was quite negative and refused to have anything to do with production plans. Once seen, however, there was a sudden shift in attitude and the group wanted full credit and control over the production, ignoring the fact that they had nothing to do with it from the beginning.

WHOSE BABY IS IT?

Luckily, our policies made the squabble irrelevant. One copy of the tape was given to the foster parent who had spearheaded the idea for his use in promoting the foster parent program. Other copies were made available at the AV desk and through the Social

Services Department for anyone wanting to use it without charge (they paid the cost of tape for the copies they circulated). As for whose baby it was, it carried the Racine Public Library logo and copyright on it, with credits going where credits were due.

The simplest way to copyright video materials, by the way, is the same way print materials are copyrighted. Show the name of the copyright holder (in our case, the name of the library) with the copyright symbol, along with the date.

It pays to copyright.

Another cooperative venture targeted children and involved a local group called the Sister Cities Committee. The committee was part of an international liaison of cities throughout the world whose citizens had formed a special bond with each other. At the time we became involved, Racine had six sister cities.

Our city librarian at the time was a member of that committee, and he suggested that we use our facilities to make a tape that illustrated the history and background of present-day Racine. This tape would then be shown to Racine's sister cities around the world, initally in Oiso, Japan, and then in the five other cities in Europe and the southern hemisphere.

WHAT TO DO WITH TOO MANY COOKS

We struggled with this project from the first. The committee wanted to do a straight documentary, aided by social studies teachers from the Unified School District. The first drafts of the script had me dozing off as I read them. It was obvious that we were dealing with the *up against the blackboard and keep the camera rolling* syndrome again. I could well imagine what this effect would do to someone trying to comprehend all those complex statistics and endless lists, especially when English was a second language, at best.

Barry and I held a council of war, desperate. Not only was the script unworkable, but it ignored the first law of video: don't tell them if you can possibly show them instead. There was simply no way to present that stuff in a visual manner. One 10 minute segment (out of what was supposed to be a 30 minute tape) was devoted, for example, to talking about local Indian tribes and the crops they raised. We would have been hard pressed to find even 30 seconds of such footage in present day Racine, where Indians are few and far between and the ones remaining generally wear Levis instead of leather. Besides, given the fact that we were trying to make a documentary about how the city grew, putting emphasis on what happened before it was established as a city seemed counter-productive.

We tried to figure out how to make the documentary interesting and still include everything that everyone wanted. Then the pro-verbial lightbulb went on over my head and I rattled off to Barry, "What if we take what we've actually got here — teachers trying to tell about Racine to students interested in learning — and we use that as an outline for our documentary. We'll get someone to play the part of a teacher, set the story in a classroom, and have a bunch of kids acting the part of students talking about Racine. The teacher can add the details that the kids don't know and there can be a lot of give and take among the actors to add variety to the information and we can put in cover shots where we have cover and leave the camera on the kids where we don't have cover and maybe that will let us get in everything we need to get in without getting bogged down in lists and statistics and ..."

Yes, I really did talk like that, and yes, that's how these things really do get done. In refining my off the cuff idea, Barry suggested putting the teacher and students in a theatre setting rather than a schoolroom for purposes of control over lighting and staging.

From past experience we knew that Jill Jensen would be the perfect person to play the teacher at her usual unpaid rate; and we were pretty sure that the Children's Theatre would be willing to suggest the names of young actors to work with us. We wanted kids of varied ethnic backgrounds and ages to show the diversity of our city and the rich heritage we would be boasting about in our video history.

In much more time than it takes to tell about it, we had a pack of children ready to take their places as mini historians, Jill had agreed to take the role of the teacher, and the Theatre Guild had agreed to let us use their facilities for taping. The script was the only prob-lem, since — though the Unified people agreed that the playlet was an excellent method of introducing the subject and would make the film more appealing to the Sister City schoolchildren to whom it was addressed — these consultants still distrusted anything that looked like fun and constantly wanted more and more lists and statistics incorporated into the tape. We held multiple meetings and finally reached the point where I would almost agree to any-thing just to get the show on the road. The script got rather ponderous at times. But thanks to our wonderful cast, it all came out sounding natural and even, Heaven help us, interesting.

HOLLYWOOD CALLING, SORT OF

Once this complex tape was edited and approved by the library and committee heads for distribution, the Sister Cities Committee set up a premiere at the Golden Rondelle Theatre, inviting all the actors and everyone involved in the production to attend. They even arranged to have miniature Oscars to present to each of our young actors. The children were delighted to receive this attention, and became the subject of front-page stories in the local newspaper telling about their adventures in making a tape that would be shown throughout the world.

It begins to get redundant, I know; but the showing was a great success, and we received many requests for the tape from everyone in town who'd read about it or knew someone who had been involved in putting it together. It was a tape we were really proud to have made, too, because, despite the constant nitpicking and second-guessing, it really was an excellent production, showing the background of our city from the point of view of everyday people, prominent businesses and local tradition simultaneously.

It had something for everyone, covering just enough of each subject to keep the momentum going without being superficial. Now that I look back at it, I'm darned if I know how we managed to get all that in. But we did. And our actors had a wonderful time doing it. That's a very important point, when it's the only currency any of them was ever going to receive for all their work.

From the very beginning, the Sister Cities Committee formed their partnership with us with a clear understanding of their responsibilities toward the cost of production. In this instance costs were fairly light since they included only the price of shooting and editing tape and dubbing copies. They were also kind enough to make photocopies of the scripts for everyone, using their facilities instead of ours, which saved us time and money.

At the time we first talked about all the possibilities of production, the committee also considered having one of the two sound tracks on each tape dubbed with a translation of the script so it could be played in the language of the country to which it would be sent. In the event that that idea panned out, we made it very clear that all such translations would be the financial responsibility of the

Committee, not the library.

We had managed to produce a worthwhile, informational piece that met a variety of needs, and we did this by utilizing a number of community resources to help us do the job. The help of the script advisors, actors and facility managers was worth thousands of dollars, and we got it for a *thank you*.

WHERE ELSE CAN YOU LOOK?

Up to this point in our production history, we had enjoyed the favor of an anonymous gift, a generous donation from the Kiwanis, and additional money from the Racine County Area Foundation. All these sources set us up with the basic equipment we needed for starting out. In the following two years, the Friends of the Library gave us a tape recorder and editing furniture to make our work easier, but we had only begun to tap the possibilities of outside funding for our work.

Before we received all these sources of help, I did some grant writing in an attempt to get money for our equipment needs. It taught me a valuable lesson: state and federal grant applications seldom pay for equipment requests unless results are focused on database creation or maintenance for system wide use. My rationalizations for video equipment funds probably seemed transparent to them.

Sometimes it takes me a while to catch on, though, and I continued to write grant proposals every year. One that I sent to the Wisconsin Humanities Committee did pay off, which made me glad that I'd had all that practice with the others.

We wanted to do a videotaped interview with former Vietnamese citizens now living in Racine. The war had been over for more than ten years and we felt it would be fascinating to examine this bit of unique modern history. My other work had gotten so time intensive at that point, however, that there was no way I could conduct the interviews and do a professional job of it. As a result of the Wisconsin Humanities Committee proposal I wrote, however, we were given a $1,000 grant to pay a local humanist, John Neuenschwander of Carthage College, to do the background search and conduct interviews.

John's unique talents made him not only a professor of history but a Kenosha County judge as well. In addition he'd authored books on oral history and the law, which put him in an excellent position to conduct the research and interviews for us. These abilities also made him one of the busiest men in the state, so we did everything we could to help him get the job done in the time he had to spare.

Our reference desk managed to dig up information on the Viet Nam war, and I made preliminary contacts with those people willing to speak on camera about their experiences. Finding these people was not easy, since these new Americans were reticent by nature, and many of them refused straight out to talk to us on tape, fearing that it might somehow injure relatives and friends left behind.

Nevertheless, we were able to set up the interviews and taping moved at a brisk rate. John's time was carefully allocated and the tapes he provided us with had little extraneous material to wade through.

They were all good. In fact, too good. My first impulse was to let it run unedited, but Barry brought me back down to earth. Nobody would sit through all of that information, no matter how dramatic or interesting it might be. Edited intelligently, the tape could bring the heart of those stories to the public and carry the message our interviewees had to tell.

SHOW AND TELL

It's not enough to make good tapes. People have to know that you've made them. When you consider all production expenses, remember to allow for the fact that your work needs to be introduced to the public and kept before their eyes in order to be useful to them. But again, you can find ways of getting publicity without spending a dime.

We used the device of premieres because, frankly, we had access to places that automatically assured us of free publicity when we showed our productions there. If you don't have such things as a Rondelle or a Festival Hall in your town, check local community theaters or see what can be done on your own premises to accommodate a crowd.

One caution: we were able to borrow corporate equipment, including projection television, enabling us to show our videotapes to a large crowd. If you must use your own facilities, plan to borrow or rent projection equipment so everyone can see and hear the tape comfortably. A standard sized television, even a large one, simply doesn't have the visibility to accommodate a crowd, and you won't be using your efforts to best advantage if you don't plan on a minimum of 100 people at your premieres. One other possibility, though an awkward one, is to station three or more large sets around a room to create separate small viewing areas.

At our premieres we invited the Mayor, city and county department heads and legislators, the press, everyone even remotely connected with the subject or production, library staff members and the public. Plan on doing the same. You'll be amazed at how many of them show up, and have a wonderful time to boot.

Be sure to have printed flyers or pamphlets to hand out at the showing, and use them as handouts in your public areas before and after all premieres. These should not only tell about the current production, but list everything else available through your facility. Hand them out shamelessly.

There's no such thing as too much exposure of your work. We loaned copies of our original tapes to the library system so they could be shown continuously at county fairs in the two county area for which we were the resource library. Needless to say, our pamphlets accompanied the tapes as pickup material. We even took our act to local malls, attracting shoppers with the video and handing out flyers to advertise the AV Department's open hours.

In the long run, you'll find that publicity pays off in terms of public interest, which has a direct impact on the type of support you can count on receiving for your productions. Also, it doesn't hurt a bit to be able to tell people that once in place, the production facility will need only the price of tape and occasional tuneups and repair of equipment to continue functioning for many years into the future.

Along with direct financial help, we also received invaluable assistance from individuals, specialized groups and several of the companies in town. When we did historical work, such as the Sister Cities tape, or filmed the performance of *Captain Knapp*, the city's founder, we were able to use the facilities of the Racine County Historical Society Museum.

They provided us with old photos and artifacts and let us use their interior displays as sets, which gave us authentic log cabin and Victorian parlor interiors. We were able to get additional footage at no cost from the local cable office when we needed it. And when we wanted to use an expensive model of the harbor project, the designers lent it to us cheerfully for as long as we needed it to tape the proposed project from several angles. There's no way to put a price tag on that kind of help. And it's the kind of help that will be available to you, wherever you are. All you have to do is ask.

To sum it all up, there are as many sources of help and funding available to you as there are people in your city. Many offers come with strings attached, however, so keep in mind just what it will really cost you as well as what benefits you'll receive when you accept.

Throughout the stories I've told about our productions a common thread that runs through all of them, in addition to gifts of money, is the constancy of free help from private citizens, from companies, and from other technicians. In the next chapter I'll tell you where your best sources of free talent lie. After all, why start spending money now?

FOUR

Talent:

Where To Get It

For Free

ALL THE WORLD'S A STAGE

If you were to put an ad in the paper asking for volunteers to act in video productions for free you might want to leave town for a while because you'd be up to your production values in eager helpers the second the ad hit the paper. In fact, after a while you'd begin to believe they were falling out of the trees. Everyone's second business, as the saying goes, seems to be Show Business.

Finding people who are willing to work for you is not the problem. The problem is finding competent, trained people who also happen to come across well on tape.

Some of the most attractive people I've seen do not seem wonderful on videotape, while others who seemed blah discovered another persona when the camera turned on. You probably won't have the luxury of doing screen tests with the people you want to work with, but sometimes you can guess which people will give you the results you're looking for.

From a purely physical standpoint, everything you've heard about cameras is true. Because of the interesting way that videotape brings the background forward, it makes people in the foreground look shorter, heavier, and sometimes even wrinklier than they are in what passes for real life. Tape is not fair.

The good part of setting up a production shoot is knowing that you are not really in show business so you don't have the worry of

ratings. In fact, most people are delighted to see familiar faces on a
television set, especially if it has something to do with their own
interests, for instance their ethnic group or fellow hobbyists; it will
grab them as nothing else would, not even Cindy Crawford in a
bikini.

Well, almost nothing else. If you are taping an expert showing
how something is done, the subject speaks for itself, and the expert
can simply be him/herself, without worrying about attractiveness.
When we interviewed people who had important things to say, it
wasn't necessary to have some blowdried news reader sit in for
them. If we encountered some stiffness or mannerisms that inter-
fered with the message, we could generally overcome the problem
by spending a little time setting them at their ease or giving them
time to calm down, forget about the camera, and just respond to
questions and the genuine interest of the interviewer. Generally,
when you do interviews with prominent people in your area, you'll
find that most of them are quite at ease with a camera rolling. The
hard part will be coming up with enough questions to elicit the responses that you need to fit into your documentary plans. Like a
lawyer conducting a cross examination, never ask a question that
you don't already know the answer to. But more of that when we
get into the chapter on preparing the script.

YOUR OWN CASTING CALL

When you're doing work that requires talent to portray a part or
memorize specific lines, you'll want to find someone with more
than public speaking experience. My first choice has always been
to look for help from the community theaters in your own area.
Chances are pretty good that you'll have a chance to see these
people in action on stage before you ever approach them to work
with you; it's even better if you have connections in community
theater of your own. I had the good fortune of working with
people from Kenosha, Racine and Milwaukee, and so I already
knew who most of the talented people were. The most appealing
thing about using community theater is the fact that you already
know these people are disciplined, enthusiastic, and prepared to
put in a lot of time and effort simply to do the work. Nobody gets
paid for acting, working the sets or gathering props. Applause is
literally the only coin they see. So volunteering to work with you
will not be a sacrifice for these actors, but an opportunity.

Don't let yourself be influenced by anyone else's opinion but your own when it comes to choosing the people who will become the image that the public sees as your organization's. Friendship often has a lot to do with it, but be sure when you ask a friend to be one of your volunteers you're sure this person can deliver when you need it. You're not in the business of giving acting lessons or making promotional tapes for movie star wannabes. Warm bodies are not enough; you have to develop an eye for putting together the project and the talent as a perfect match.

IN YOUR LAP

Sometimes this match comes ready made, and you can still include friendship in the deal. When we made the videotape about the life of Racine's founder, the perfect cast was already in place, and it was their skill and talent that suggested the project in the first place.

During the city's celebration of its sesquicentennial year a couple prominent in local community theater, Jim and Vi Yorgan, were asked by the Sesquicentennial Committee to portray Captain Gilbert Knapp and his wife. This lively pair embraced the concept and appeared at civic events, schools and churches as the Knapps, telling the story of the city's founding to hundreds of delighted Racinians. Since I was acquainted with the Yorgans both as actors and as friends, I knew that they could deliver the goods. I also knew that their appearances were wildly popular wherever they went.

The past took on full life as the Yorgans, dressed in authentic costumes researched and sewn by Vi herself, gave uncanny portrayals based on facts they themselves researched and verified. This was a perfect example of free talent: the script, costumes, actors and built-in audience fell into our laps, and the fact that the Yorgans were also friends of mine helped a lot when it came to asking them to recreate their roles before our cameras.

If you look carefully around your own city, you will find celebrations exactly like this one, with history and celebration linked to a visually exciting concept. Every place has a founder's story, every place has a history that can be told in a less than awful way. There may not be nine million stories in your town, but there are more than enough to keep you filling tape for years to come without running dry should you choose to specialize in local history.

One reason the Yorgans' performances were so popular is that they behaved so naturally and were so at ease that they were able to answer questions from the audience as if they actually were the Knapps returned to life. It was totally untheatrical; if not for the costumes, they might have been contemporary visitors talking to the crowds. It was only when they pulled out dates and incidents from the past that the audience would remember this was an act. Their Knapp personas seemed completely natural.

In fact, at one point, they went into a little pseudo argument about something that happened after Knapp's death, and the "widow" interrupted his monologue with the observation that he hadn't actually been around to see this event; his response was that he had indeed been there, just not in the flesh, so to speak. Children loved that line, and it seemed that adults felt a tinge of wry amusement when they heard it. If it was wishful thinking, it was the kind that rang a bell with all ages, and our actors were canny enough to know it. Sometimes instinct works better than careful scripting.

Despite the popularity of their touring show, however, during the entire sesquicentennial year not one of their performances had been put on film or tape, though hundreds of people had seen it in person and segments had been shown on live local televison. It wasn't until the following year we discovered this oversight and asked them to put their performances on tape for us.

It required a bit of backtracking for the Yorgans to recreate their performances after all that while, but they pitched right in, polished their lines, dusted off their costumes and were raring to go.

The question of *where* to go arose; this version of the Knapps' story would be considerably different, since there would not be an audience to carry the narration forward and keep the sense of spontaneity going. They had to take all their anecdotes and play off each other to get the points across that they used to bounce off a crowd of eager onlookers. It was going to be much harder to make a bare stage credible when everything else about the story — narrative, costumes and appearance — was totally realistic.

ANOTHER FREEBIE

In looking at various alternatives, we considered our local Historical Society Museum, whose second floor was made up of full-size room displays behind floor to ceiling glass. These displays recreated scenes from life in early Racine complete with authentic 1830's furniture and artifacts. To our delight, when we asked for permission to use these rooms during closed hours for the Museum, the director agreed. He allowed us to tape the "Knapps" inside these glass walled sets, which provided us with two essential backgrounds.

The first was an authentic log cabin interior. It had hand hewn log walls, spinning wheel, furniture and even clothing true to the era that hung on the wall pegs. The second set was an elegant Victorian parlor, much like the one in which the Knapps really lived out their lives as first citizens of the town. We had a horsehair sofa for them to sit on, a fireplace with massive mantel and hardware to match, and a prop that gave us pause. It was a small stuffed dog, rather seedy and definitely long departed. We didn't write a part for him, and mostly worked around his presence on the set. You don't really have to use everything you're given, even if it is free.

And what we got for free was considerable: a first-class narrative already written and verified historically; two experienced performers willing to donate their time and effort to put it on tape for us; and a museum with authentic sets showing exactly the period we needed to reproduce. Everything seemed to be handed to us on a platter. The only touch we as a production crew added was to tape footage of the monument over Gilbert Knapp's grave as background for the credits. And even there, Nature gave us a freebie. It turned out to be a beautiful sunlit day when we went to the historic cemetery, and the grave marker looked magnificent against that bright blue sky. Or was that Gilbert's contribution?

HOW TO DO A HOW TO

Another instance of having an idea handed to us involved the taping of a very popular children's program. The teaching of origami, or Japanese paperfolding, was a subject much in demand when programs were set up for the Children's Department of the library. This translated into a perfect idea for a *how to* tape, thanks to the fact that the lively Japanese lady who gave the children's programs for free was willing to do the same on videotape. In this case, the instructor was fully at home with her subject, had presented it before eager crowds many times, and was not uncomfortable in front of the camera. She was also tiny, soft spoken and completely charming, attributes that showed up on tape. Dressed in her traditional kimono, she could not only demonstrate the techniques of origami, but had the background and knowledge to provide insights into its history and uses.

Keep in mind that we were also working from the point of view of a traditional library; we not only recorded interesting, useful material, but also created productions with built in archival value. In the two examples cited above, we built archival elements directly into the final tape. You may find that this approach works for your needs, too. It's a definite plus for many Boards when they justify this activity as a line item in the budget.

For the Knapp tape, in addition to the obvious historic value of the story itself , we concluded the tape with an interview with the actors at the end of their performance so that viewers gained additional background information on the city's sesquicentennial celebration itself, finding out about the people involved in that civic celebration, and even learning about what it was like to live in Racine in the 1980's as well as the 1830's.

In the origami instructional tape, our narrator embellished her directions with commentary on the history of the art, its origins, what place it held in present-day Japanese customs and how each of the completed pieces was intended to be used. It was essentially painless education for adults and children alike. And again, the entire program and its talented performer were a package that we had only to frame with our camera.

WHEN TO LEAVE IT ALONE

But we also taped many interviews containing strong archival elements in their raw state, including details and commentary that expanded on the subject under consideration. While we simply could not, for production purposes, release unedited interviews as a finished product, we did save all original raw tapes and placed them in the safekeeping of our archival librarian to be made available to serious scholars and historians with an interest in complete, unedited commentaries. In this way we fulfilled our obligation to history in a dual manner, providing an entertaining overview of the subjects we approached as well as the research that went into it. It might have been an ethnic group's contribution to our community or the process behind the harbor development that became a structured, complete documentary, while we could leave a more definitive, less structured record exactly as it was taped, for those whose scholastic needs required a verbatim record.

If you look around your town , especially in your own library or school, you'll see that certain things appeal to a particular audience, as much as did the performances of the Yorgans or the origami demonstrations that turn bits of paper into birds and other delight-ful things. You'll manage to discover subjects of interest to many people simply by being aware of what they show up to see. And for the most part, if the person who presents the program does so for free, your chances of getting them to do it on tape for free are excellent. The time and energy required for taping these activities are minimal as well, depending on how elaborately you choose to produce them.

In the case of the Yorgans' tape, for example, we planned to complete the shoot in two days. This allowed time for setting up and cleaning up our sets, which were, in this case, the display rooms in the museum. We had to fit our taping plans within their schedule so that we wouldn't interfere with public access. It was essential that we took responsibility for making the taping sessions as easy on our hosts as we could. We also had to be sensitive to the amount of time our actors were giving us. Two days was a very large chunk out of their busy lives.

When it came time to do the origami tape, we simply set up a table in our meeting room and used that for our set. We seldom stopped the tape, since Keiko Skow, our origami instructor, was an experienced, fast performer. Children's attention spans had honed her art well, and she required no props outside of cut paper for demonstrations and her finished items. Since the attention of our potential audience would be focused tightly on the process being demonstrated, background was of minimal importance.

BORROWING WORKS

Another more important reason we saved shooting time with the origami tape was the fact that we were able to borrow a second camera. All those connections we made with the video community continued to pay off despite the lack of formal meetings and organ-izational structure. We called one of our neighborhood video producers and found that we could use their camera for the day, at no cost, of course. It was a reciprocal agreement, meaning that when they needed a second camera to expedite a shoot, we would oblige with ours.

Putting Barry on one camera and me on the other, we were able to tape two simultaneous views as we went along; the first camera concentrated on closeups while the other showcased our performer with a wider range of perspectives, sometimes moving in to a medium shot, sometimes moving out to a wide one. In that way we had both tapes when we edited the piece so we could cut in the closeups as needed to insure that the demonstration was easy to follow.

If you wanted to accomplish the same effect using a single camera, you'd have to repeat the demonstration at least twice, using the camera for a broader perspective in one session and moving in for closeups in another.

As a matter of fact, we sometimes had to do just that when the script called for such versatility and we weren't able to borrow a spare camera. Needless to say, we tried to avoid shoots that called for duplication of time and effort. It simply cost too much in terms of patience, besides adversely affecting the spontaneity we worked towards.

Even allowing for time spent in post-production work, you can see that these two tapes are perfect examples of a fast, low budget method of producing videotapes to satisfy a variety of uses. Schools, especially, found the tapes fit in well with their curriculum needs. But other patrons took them home, too, some to enjoy learning new things, and some to refresh their memories of having seen the live performances. And in the case of demonstration tapes, the capacity to stop the action or repeat it at will made that instruction infinitely valuable to someone learning a new skill.

CHECK THOSE YELLOW PAGES

Once we were up and running with our productions, the word went out to the community that we were adding some interesting material to our AV desk. People came to us with ideas for additional possibilities; we even received offers from local florists and lumberyards to help us film how-to videos on projects ranging from flower arranging to caring for bonsai trees to building wooden decks and furniture. Producing tapes like these would require little time to film and edit, while public interest would have been high. Remember, at that time there were no *This Old House* or *Yankee Craftsman* shows offering help to fledgling handicrafters.

Still, even with the wealth of programming available for purchase today, consider the powerful effect on your viewers to see familiar faces on the television screen. That effect can make local productions popular with, and truly helpful to, your own audience. When your patron decides to follow through on a project, it's convenient to know that everything discussed on the tape will be readily available close at hand, not to mention that the demonstrator on the tape will probably be able to answer questions in person!

Should you feel that this is a possible use for your production facilities, consider approaching some of the more skilled artisans in your town. From my own experience I'd say that the reaction will be favorable, and of course there's the additional touch of having local businesses provide you with free publicity.

It might be wise to deal with a number of people in each of the areas being considered for production, rather than concentrating on just one. The reason for this is, of course, that if you use one florist for flower arranging, you may want to have a second florist to give directions for bonsai and still another to show how to prepare outdoor flower beds. It avoids the implication that your organization is showing favoritism towards a particular merchant, and it also lets each specialist concentrate on that specialty, providing truly expert instruction for your patrons. Yes, favoritism sounds political. That's why you can't afford to get involved in anything that has even the faintest whiff of it.

Another idea we were considering was that of putting general information about real estate sales and purchases, general advice about when to seek legal help, or the nuts and bolts of pursuing higher education on tape, using a kind of *ask the expert* approach to the subjects.

These possibilities were suggested by the people who could provide the talent; while seminars on these topics had proved to be highly popular, they needed to be more flexible for people who needed to work at their own pace. Just as the library made books in those subject areas available to patrons, so could it do with videotaped specialized advice.

Working with professionals in the field also insures that you won't violate any ethical standards while providing general advice to guide people in finding out when to seek more specific — and expensive — help.

DOING YOUR OWN THING

When it came to finding talent for the tapes we initiated ourselves, we found ourselves in a totally different position than when the program came to us as a gift package. In one case, our library director wanted a tape produced to hype the benefits of library services for the whole community. We had already designed one tape with a hard sell edge to it; very straightforwardly, we used the format of having an actress walk through the obviously overcrowded library while explaining the need for additional space. Strictly show and tell. That approach worked in that case, but we knew going in that a hard sell was not going to work for us here.

We had to think about what library patrons themselves would consider to be benefits, and we had to show those benefits from a patron's point of view. We had to move outside our own vantage point and into theirs if we were to tell the true story effectively. So we did two things before even outlining a script: we talked to the staff, and we talked to some of our regular patrons. This is the kind of advice that a consultant could charge big bucks for, and you can use it, too. For free, as we did.

From the staff's observations we learned which services were most used and commented on by various segments of our users. From the patrons, we learned about the deep feelings many people have, some of them going back to childhood, about what libraries mean to them. In many cases these feelings colored their every contact with a library as adults even when there was no correlation between past and present experiences.

There were people who had had warm, fuzzy experiences as children in their first contacts with a library; there were also those who had never been inside a friendly library as a child, whose parents didn't know or care enough to give them a positive experience with libraries, and who were therefore hostile — or at least uncomfortable — with the prospect of dealing with them as adults. And there were people who claimed with a straight face that they never used libraries, had no use for libraries, and didn't understand what the big deal was, even when their secretaries or children called our reference desk several times a day for essential information.

Once we had this insight and had taken the time to analyze it we began to outline what we wanted to present on tape. We took that outline to the Librarian and department heads for refinement.

From this consensus I developed a script that I hoped would address the things we needed to talk about.

The finished script used the voices of two people, a man and a woman, who would not be seen on screen but who would carry the narrative forward. We also planned to tape closeups of patrons, librarians and circulation people combined with longer shots of the general public using our services. By the time we had it shaped up it looked like we'd need a cast of thousands.

The proposed size of the cast was not our only problem. In addition to using actual staff members who had long since given up hope that we'd stop dragging them into these things, we also needed the sense of authenticity that could only come from using real patrons talking about real experiences. If you've ever listened to a truly bad interview you have some idea of the problems this posed. Most people are capable of being quite articulate, and even moving, in expressing their views — as long as there isn't a camera staring them in the face.

We went back to the circulation staff for help once more. This time we asked them for the names of patrons who were particularly self-confident and who expressed positive feelings about the library. We thought we'd have a problem filling that bill, but it was amazing to see how many people our staffers could pinpoint for us. The rapport between staff and public had always been a warm one, and this indirect PR was paying off for us now that we needed to cash in on it.

Our next step was to contact these people and get them to agree not only to speak on camera, but to work from a written script. We needed to use a script because things that work well in an oral history interview could backfire in a production designed to promote library usage. Ramblings, stammering or self-conscious behavior of any kind would all make viewers painfully aware that these patrons were talking to a camera and not to them. At the same time, the script had to reflect actual feelings and experiences or it would ring a false note worse than simple awkwardness.

It took a couple of weeks to contact chosen patrons, discuss the script with those willing to help, and set up convenient times for taping their segments.

INFORMED CONSENT

I have to make a small aside at this point: every time we used someone who was identifiable in one of our productions we asked them to sign a consent form giving us permission to use the tape for library archival purposes. That might sound sinister, but it merely insures that everyone on both sides of the agreement understands the process. It's exactly what still photographers do when people in published photos give permission for their images to be used. In the case of video, a little more complex understanding was required.

For example, one of the key phrases incorporated into our consent forms was "subject to editing." We explained at the time the form was signed that what we had on raw tape probably would not appear in the finished production exactly as shot.

It was important for people to understand that there could be many reasons to change what appeared on the tape before it was incorporated into a finished production. Most of them had heard about the cutting room floor and understood that things might be changed for a number of good reasons. While we generally didn't cut segments following a script, it was always possible that we might have to trim or rearrange portions of it, possibly to change the pace or eliminate whatever didn't quite work. It was almost a certainty that we would edit down portions of general interviews simply because the nature of an interview calls for repetitious questions and a broad variety of approaches to achieve enough information to fit into the proposed tape.

Also, in even the most wonderful, succinct interview, people have been known to make peculiar faces or sneeze or do other things that they would prefer not to display to the general public. To be fair, camera operators have also been known to blow it, making out of focus shots at a crucial moment. Whatever the reason, timing or accident, few interviews can be left to run without some trimming.

But it has to be made perfectly clear to people that their words are subject to editing, that portions of their statement might not appear when the tape is finished. Telling them upfront avoids hurt feelings or confusion, and getting a signed release also puts your institution in a good spot in the unlikely event that your subject dislikes the finished product. While we never had a problem, it's a good rule to follow and it will make your city attorney very happy if you do. You can create your own release form with very little effort or you can use the following as a model if you wish:

RELEASE FORM

I, _____, agree to allow the
                    (name)

_____
              (your library/agency/etc.)

to use videotape on which I appear for the following production:

_____;

I understand that this production may be subject to editing as

required for viewing by the general public.

Name _____   Date _____

Address _____

Name of employee witnessing signature

_____

Your legal advisors may prefer to come up with something
more elaborate to cover various contingencies, but essentially you
are simply asking for permission to use — and if necessary, alter —
the tape on which the person appears. It's a minor point, but one
that comes under the heading of Protective Management.

THE PERFECT PICTURE

Getting back to putting production and talent together, let's
consider the sources we used to complete the library video. In this
instance we used the widest variety of sources we had ever tapped:

staff, patrons, friends, and in at least two instances, relatives. They turned out to be great fun to work with. And they were all naturals.

In one memorable spot, a friend who had had some public relations training played the role of a young mother describing the joy of sharing stories she loved as a child with her three-year-old daughter. The words were essentially her own, as were the sentiments. Only the script was ours.

Like her mother, the little girl was completely relaxed on camera, responding to her mother's cues without the slightest hesitation. It rang true because it expressed the mother's actual feelings and experiences. We just put it into words that were easy to say and reflected the point of view we wanted to express on the video.

To read the part of the background narrator, we asked a high school English teacher with community theater experience to be our male voice. He had a rich, warm baritone that added much to his performance. His wife, also a teacher/actress, was to have provided us with the companion voice, but other obligations prevented it. I hastily pulled my daughter into the breach, since her voice most closely approximated the warm soprano we needed for balance. To keep it all in the family, I also enlisted my grandson for a non-speaking part as a young motorcyclist. His acting partner in that scene was a bearded department head who managed to look convincing as a tough cycle rider seeking information at the reference desk. Yes, we do get creative when we need to keep people's attention on the screen.

We ran into an interesting challenge in taping the narrators and we solved it in an equally interesting way. During the taping we ran a sound check and discovered that they were coming across rather flat because of the acoustics in the editing room.

To give more depth to their voices we moved them into the AV department's tiny washroom and tested the sound again. It was perfect. But we had to allow for a certain amount of giggling before we could complete the tape, since the two of them found the prospect of recording the script while jammed together in a cramped, dark bathroom pretty bizarre.

The room was dark because we discovered that when the light switch was turned on, it triggered a loud exhaust fan which drowned out their voices. So in addition to working in tight quarters, they also had to read by incidental light coming through the open door. Talk about dedication.

PUTTING THE TOWN ON TAPE

We used a lot of different people for non-speaking roles in this tape. We took the approach that people are not aware of the services they take for granted, by definition. Sometimes they needed a little consciousness raising. To illustrate some of those services, we shot footage of a mail carrier delivering letters; a waitress pouring coffee in a popular restaurant; and a bakery clerk packaging up one of our town's most popular products, a kringle. It was an easy connection between these and the circulation and reference desks at the library as two more services that people took for granted — a worthwhile and necessary part of everyday life.

It was time-consuming and complicated to set up all these scenes, but once they were lined up the taping itself went surprisingly fast. Even better, the editing was simple since most of the work had been done in the scripting. It's a good deal easier to have the exact words ahead of time so that you know where they're going to appear and how they will fit into the whole picture.

We melded the individual scenes together with the background voices and found ourselves with a 20-minute tape that held all the elements called for: real patrons talking about real benefits presented to them by a real library. It's the sort of tape that any library could show with pride, and the soft sell approach was designed to appeal to patrons everywhere.

GUIDING THE SPONTANEOUS

Using real people and scripted commentary worked for us this time, but there are many instances when you just can't put words in other people's mouths. When you're doing interviews that require factual, individual responses, the best you can do is ask questions designed to elicit answers that should fit within a loosely scripted outline. This is where those repetitious questions come in.

The oral histories were a perfect example of this, but so was the tape that we made on the Festival Park. We had to go with both scripted and spontaneous statements for the latter production. I asked questions of people involved in the project and we taped the replies. It was only after we scanned the interviews that we could determine what parts of the story needed clarification through a scripted narrative.

We added a host to carry the story forward logically and pro-

vide information not contained in the interviews. This narration
helped to link portions of the tape and move them smoothly into a
seamless whole. To achieve this meant finding the right narrator,
of course. And after asking around and discussing the situation,
we found the perfect person to do the job. Jean Jacobson was on
the County Board and had an intimate knowledge of the project.
She also had a pleasant, relaxed manner, an attractive appearance,
and the willingness to put those attributes at our disposal.

ASK FOR WHAT YOU NEED — YOU JUST MIGHT GET IT

In every one of the cases I've been describing people were more
than willing to give us their time without charge. In fact, some of
them were more than delighted to have a forum for their own
stories about the subject at hand. Don't disdain such insights; they
are often serendipitous treasures that lend a whole new flavor and
liveliness to your story. While you certainly want to follow the
story line as you've written it, an occasional sidelight can add a
touch of freshness just when you need it.

In the process of making oral histories, on the other hand, there
are other considerations that need to be taken into account. First of
all it's a great deal easier to create these tapes if you have some
outside help in deciding who should be included in the narrative.
The broader the perspective you're dealing with — i.e., black history, local architecture — the more expert help you will need to
narrow your target area down to a workable approach. Otherwise,
you can walk into a minefield of problems.

Some of those problems can be political. When we were doing
preparatory work for our Black oral history tape, our first approach
was to make a list of names that were most familiar to us through
personal acquaintance, newspaper stories or other publicity. In our
ignorance we assumed that those would be the people most likely
to contribute to oral history with significant, memorable anecdotes.

Our plans were given a sharp right turn when we sought the
help of a committee of local African American leaders who met
with us and gave us the benefit of their advice. Our trouble with
politics reared its head when we learned that the most familiar
names were not necessarily the people most representative of the
Black experience in Racine. Choosing the wrong side could alien-
ate others in the city, and we had no way of knowing, from the
opinions we were getting, which side could possibly be the *right*

one. If we'd thought about it, of course, we'd have realized that
Elton John and Queen Elizabeth might get a lot of press in Britain,
but that doesn't make them especially representative of the average
British citizen.

Not only that, but the most vocal and visible people are not
always the ones who can tell the kind of smaller, more intimate,
personal stories that make up the basis of oral history. We were not
looking for superstars, after all, but for ordinary people whose
experiences would strike resonant chords in others. We were looking for that "Oh, yes, I remember that!" response. If the memories
rang true, they could also give younger viewers accurate insights
into the way things used to be.

So there we were, trying to compile a list of ordinary people
we'd never heard of. That did seem to be carrying it a bit too far;
so we compromised and instead asked for suggestions about
people who had done something they really wanted to do with
their lives, something that made them at once ordinary and special.
Within those parameters, we were able to come up with categories,
and from those categories we formulated a tentative list of names.

There are always more suggestions than there are people willing to tell their stories on videotape. This may seem like a conun-
drum, but actually it's the best possible way to get a good mix. If
we had managed to get the people we first went after, we would
have missed the unexpected excitement of hearing stories that were
brand new to us but which echoed in the Black community like a
well tuned blues note.

In the process of choosing our categories we considered several
clergymen because of their high profiles, but it could have been a
serious misstep to choose one over another. Instead, we asked their
advice on what approach to take and were rewarded with a sugges-
tion to tape the life story of a retired teacher/administrator whose
bootstrap rise in local education still impacts on minority children
in Racine today.

On the other hand, I used my own judgment in taping the story
of a militant Black Muslim I met through the AV desk. He was a
teacher at an alternative school whose opinions about whites were
supposedly well known and contemptuous.

However, in the time I'd gotten to know him I caught the sug-
gestion of a more complex story. I asked if he would like to participate in our tape. He agreed, not to expound on his militant views
but to share the story of his childhood, so similar to that of many

others in the city. He had grown up as the son of a sharecropper, and he told the tale of his growing up years with a disarming sweetness and warmth.

Because religion is such an important part of Black community life in Racine, we felt that it needed to be represented. Since we had chosen to eliminate the clergy as a subject, we came up with the idea of interviewing a couple whose everyday lives were transformed when they became gospel singers. Their children added voices and instruments to the group as they grew up. We found a warmth and sincerity in their narrative which was taped as a simple conversation between husband and wife discussing something they felt strongly about.

Part of the charm of this interview came from the comic moments that emerged, often when they offered deadpan corrections to each other about small points the way married people tend to do. It added a warm human touch. But their conversations also contained home truths that became even more apparent to me when I listened to the first audience that saw it. Soft whispers of "Yeah" and "Amen" burst out almost unconsciously. They had the unmistakable ring of recognition, the very thing we were seeking when we first chose the stories we would tell.

SOMETIMES THE ANSWER IS NO

When we looked for people to interview for the Vietnamese video we ran into a different series of obstacles. For many reasons, particularly the strong emotions still elicited by memories of the war, people were not anxious to break cover and call attention to themselves and their experiences. We still encountered the bitterness on both sides about the way the war had whimpered to a halt, leaving so many Vietnamese stranded by their allegiance to the United States and so many Americans angry about our participation or stunned by our defeat.

We found one resource in the person of a young Vietnamese student working at the library. He was soft spoken, pleasant, and disarmingly honest when we asked him about the possibility of approaching the Vietnamese community for spokespeople to interview. His reply was that there was no such thing as a community of his compatriots in our area. There were no leaders. There were just families, some of which were couples, or in his case, simply two brothers who had banded together to support each other.

Most of them had family members still in Viet Nam, and it was this concern, added to the prejudice they had experienced in the past ten years, that made them quite reticent in calling attention to themselves. It was only when we assured them that there would be no political questions asked that we were able to get a few of them to talk to us.

Quite frankly, politics was the last thing on my mind when we set out to do the tape, but it proved to be the one overriding concern of the people we interviewed. Once they understood our purpose — to show the human side of the refugee question — they relaxed and became quite open in telling their stories. To this day, I can't watch with dry eyes the segment that Kiet taped for us, when he was trying to find words to describe how it was for him as the war destroyed not only his country, but his future. He said, "The people had their bodies there, but they had no souls."

Because this was the story to be told, it would have been the height of folly to choose a narrative script, or actors, to give these experiences life. The words had to come directly from those who experienced them. We will always be grateful to those who fought off still one more kind of fear to share those memories with us.

SOMETIMES YOU GET MORE THAN YOU PAY FOR

The one part of this experience that didn't come under the heading of free talent was, of course, the humanist/historian we hired to do the interviews. John Neuenschwander was paid, as mentioned earlier, by money from a grant given through the Wisconsin Humanities Committee, and considering the hours of work he put in, he more than earned his fee.

It's not always possible to get a nationally known expert to contribute to your work for free, so keep in mind that there are other ways to accomplish this without putting your organization out of pocket. On the other hand, there is the factor we in the business call dumb luck.

The library had been talking to a local environmentalist group about doing a documentary showcasing Chiwaukee Prairie, one of the last true prairies left in our part of the midwest. Its name was a distillation of the names *Chicago* and *Milwaukee*, since the land lay between the two, just inside Kenosha County near the Racine County line. The Chiwaukee Preservation group we were talking to was made up of people from both communities.

In order to do justice to a subject like Chiwaukee it was not enough to write a script and have local environmentalists give their point of view. When you're dealing with something of scientific value, you need credible scientists to present it properly. This is where the element of luck came in. We discovered that there would be a symposium held at the University of Wisconsin-Parkside (Kenosha) campus featuring scientists from all over the country. Their purpose was to discuss the value of preserving prairie lands, with Chiwaukee as their chosen example.

Naturally, our local preservation group was invited to be part of the symposium, and they used their entree to schedule interviews for us with the top scientists appearing there. Those gentlemen not only cut into their schedules to allow us hours of taping time, but they also brought charts and other documentation to illustrate their comments.

It was early Fall, and the weather, up to that weekend, had been warm and pleasant. In fact, it had been downright hot right until the very moment we set up our equipment in the beautifully wooded campus setting. At that point the winds picked up and the temperature dropped twenty degrees.

So there we were, in the still bright sunlight, being blown away by gusts of cold air, trying to hold down our equipment and reassure our speakers that their words could still be heard over the rustle of trees and bushes in the background. Thanks to the little round wind protectors on the lapel microphones this proved to be absolutely true.

In fact, it was almost uncanny to look at the raw tape afterwards and hear those voices, crisp and clear, without a bit of wind distortion. In the background, trees and foliage were moving like waves on a stormy sea, but the speakers might just as well have been inside for all the noise the microphones picked up.

And why didn't we go inside, you ask? We had two reasons, one of them practical, and one of them aesthetic. From the practical point of view, we had done a site survey earlier and determined that we had access to outdoor power sources near the buildings, so we didn't pack our light kit. The day was bright and perfect for an outdoor shoot. From the aesthetic viewpoint, we felt that a documentary lauding the value of the outdoors might lose credibility if it was filmed inside a building. Something could be lost in the tone, we were sure.

And so we interviewed these experts, filmed descriptive shots of the prairie itself, and melded them all together into a worthwhile documentary. This was one of those rare times when we didn't use a script but instead used the excellent statements given us to bring continuity to the story. Since they were the experts, we had only to present their talks in a coherent way and illustrate them with shots of their subject. Barry outdid himself with closeups of the tiny plants and creatures that existed on the prairie, including one wonderful shot of an industrious bee who may never have heard of Emily Dickinson but was following her advice to the letter just the same.

Afterwards, we invited the group to review our tape before we released it to the public so they could critique and if necessary correct our finished product. They took this request seriously, and took notes. They requested some minor changes in the subtitles on parts of the tape, but other than that we were assured it was a satisfactory presentation. Our experts, too, had requested copies of the tape, and received them as our thanks for participating. Because of its balanced view, they would be using the tape in classes at the university level.

Privately, we felt reassured that we had not gotten onto the advocate's bandwagon when we heard some grumbling about how our tape had shown the value of prairies but had not gone far enough in demanding that they be preserved. We tried to follow basic library principles, which meant providing all the facts, at least as far as they could be shown, and then letting people make their own decisions on whether or not to be advocates. Having the scientists present their professional views was a bonus and one that was necessary to create the type of program we wanted.

JUST THE FACTS, MA'AM

Another example of using experts to tell a story was the documentary the library did on the festival site and marina project. In this case, we could have gone either way.

The facts could be shown easily enough. We could have used a voice-over explaining the action shown on construction footage and kept it strictly business; and it was just as possible to create a "touchy-feely" kind of story with lots of music and pretty pictures.

But we wanted more. We wanted to show the story behind the pictures, hoping to illuminate far more than just the building process. Showing how the idea started, the obstacles that had to be

overcome, and how unlikely bedfellows came to work harmoni-
ously together would in turn give insight to further changes
planned between the city and county governments. Understanding the intelligent effort that had gone into these plans would, we
hoped, ground viewers on the story behind the story.

It was that quest that sent us out to interview two mayors, two
county executives, a city planner, the head of the downtown redevelopment group, and others whose legislative and personal efforts
had meshed together to bring an impossible project to fruition.

The best part about going after stories like this is that you can
experience a serendipitous effect. There is always a wonderful
story that someone recalls; there is always the look on the face of
the person telling a story when they get to the really good part; and
there is that urge to cheer when you've heard about the things that
went wrong, or threatened to go wrong, and then you see tape of a
speaker literally crowing as he welcomes the first people ever into
the new Festival Hall, just as we saw the director of the Downtown
Redevelopment Group do.

These are things that can't be done through a script, or through
storytelling. These are things that can only be shown by the people
who lived them, telling us just how it was. The excitement is shared
through the voices and faces of real people telling real stories, and
that's probably why I enjoyed every minute of producing these
tapes. No amount of work, no amount of fatigue were enough to
outweigh the joy of that ultimate moment when we shared the
finished story with an audience and saw their delight and understanding grow as it ran.

BACK TO THE DRAWING BOARD

When we did the Sister Cities project or the tape about homework research methods for school children, the fact that we had
totally different purposes for those tapes didn't mean that we
couldn't use the same methods to produce both of them. It was not
necessary to get interviews for these projects. We knew what we
wanted to say, and the best way to say it was through actors taking
those pages of dialogue and bringing them to life.

The bottom line in projects like these is control. We needed to
control the content and the timing. Unlike previous tapes that
depended on real people saying things in their own way, we had a
more general message to tell that was not dependent on the singu-

larity of experience involved. Yet we wanted to make the tapes more than just another lecture on film. The lead characters, such as they were, had to be people that our viewers would identify and feel empathy with.

That was our first clue. We went back to basics and reviewed just who our targets were. In both cases the audience would be children, though of different grade levels and ages. Who speaks to children better than their peers, we decided? And then we went off in search of children to act in these productions.

In Racine, the Theatre Guild has built a reputation for doing community theater with professional level productions. Naturally our first thoughts went to these actors, who met our most important criteria: they were experienced, talented and used to working for nothing.

But this time we needed actors who would be a bit younger than those we usually worked with. It was pure luck that there was a Children's Theatre associated with the Guild, in which young children were trained in theatrical skills. Bingo, we said. The director of the Children's Theatre provided us with names of a dozen kids who had stage presence, experience and the right amount of chutzpah to carry off our storyline.

If you think that you can just round up a group of children off the street or out of a schoolroom and have them perform for you, just take your camera some day and walk around in one of those settings. Give young passersby scripts to read from and tell them to take it seriously. Be sure to take along a large bottle of aspirin.

While today's students seem to have developed a great deal of self confidence when faced with the prospect of going on stage or on camera, it still takes a bit of experience to be able to perform on cue as needed. Of all the luxuries we lacked, the most consistent one was time. And time is the one thing that is always lost when you have to get people used to a camera. Interviews are spontaneous and therefore have a bit more leeway to them, but when you're dealing with a script that must be followed closely you need people with experience.

If there is no Children's Theatre or its equivalent in your town, ask for help from school teachers. They're in a wonderful spot to help you find dependable young actors. That's what we did for our research tape. We needed a boy and girl of high school age to whip out credible performances in a matter of days. Teachers who deal with student actors have had sufficient experience to know who can come through in a pinch and who can't. Trust them. Experience is on their side.

In the case of the two teenagers who did our research tape, I can only beat the same old drum again. They were wonderful. They grasped the situation, they didn't fool around, they were cheerful and followed direction beautifully. And they remembered their lines, though video is a forgiving medium and retakes are not always major problems.

While we're on the subject, you might just take a closer look at those teachers themselves when seeking experienced talent. If you read the biographical lines in community theater programs, you'll always find a disproportionate number of teachers on the list.

I think there's a good reason for this. Most teachers, if they're good at what they do, have learned to read their audiences and present material in varied and inventive ways. They are performing every day, and they are always looking for methods to improve those performances.

Most of them have also learned the basic skill that's most helpful to an effective teacher. They've learned to speak up clearly and loudly with voices that can carry over the muffled whispers of fifth graders, just as actors' voices must carry over the crackling of paper-wrapped candies in little old ladies' purses.

TO SCRIPT OR NOT TO SCRIPT

When you're considering sources of talent for your productions, start with asking what kind of tape you're planning to do. That answer almost always tells you what your next step will be. If you are telling a generic story, you can bring in a controlled script and choose from a wide variety of actors, those working in the theater, teachers, your own staff, schoolchildren, patrons and even family, as you've seen us do.

If you are doing a documentary your main concern will be with credibility, and you must do your best to get professionals in the field or people with direct experience using the interview process. You may or may not choose to add the services of a narrator to tie it all together, but first of all get the help of people who know what they're talking about. It's the difference between a professional piece of work and home video.

Do your homework, and be sure you know exactly what connection each of your potential interviewees has with the subject at hand, or what he or she has contributed to the subject. Most of the time the people you approach will be more than happy to provide you with suggestions for others to contact whose information would be helpful to you. And often they will want to know up front just who else is being interviewed in connection with the story. You'd better be able to answer that. If you fail to do your homework, you'll never be able to come up with intelligent questions or sniff out an interesting lead to follow. You'll also make it clear that you are following no one else's agenda but your own.

If you go in with a sincere attitude and demonstrate the best you can that you have no axe to grind, you'll find very few people who refuse to cooperate with you. Oral histories are one obvious exception to that rule, since you're asking for more than just information. You're getting very personal, and everyone has the right to refuse to share their thoughts and experiences.

Even then, if you can convince them that you won't intrude into areas they hold private, you should be able to convince a sufficient number of people to cooperate to create a well rounded project.

Finally, as we've seen, there are some subjects that come as a package deal. Programs shown at libraries or schools are interesting to many people and come readymade to be taped. It can be an easy to do but valuable production if the performers don't object to putting their acts on tape for you. When they do agree, you have everything you need handed to you: purpose, audience and performer, complete with "script" and point of view. All you have to do, essentially, is turn on the camera and shoot.

In addition to performers, however, you will find yourself in need of other kinds of help as you move into video production. Luckily, you don't have to know everything. You can use the old librarian's axiom: just know where to look for the answers.

This is true in terms of scripting probably more than anything else. If you have come up with an idea yourself, chances are that you have some background information on the subject, or you wouldn't have been interested in the first place. But if the subject is not your own idea, you have to do some digging. Since time is always tight it pays to have some notions of where to get help.

SEE YOUR LIBRARIAN

Libraries, of course, have the ultimate solution — a reference desk. Even if you're not working out of a library, you still have access to them in your community. Public libraries are especially helpful, but college libraries can provide you with specialized information in narrower fields. Still, the best solution of all, at least from a producer's point of view, would be to find someone who will do the research for you.

That's not as hard as it sounds. For example, when we were doing the tape for the Sister Cities Committee, we had members of the Unified School District's social studies department to help us determine just which elements of the city's history we should include, and they kept a close eye on the balance, to make sure that one thing didn't receive more emphasis than another. If we mentioned the businesses that started in Racine, we also mentioned the churches, museums and recreational areas. If we mentioned climate, we also mentioned ethnic diversity. When you're trying to paint a full canvas, it helps to have someone else standing back and looking for missed or fuzzy areas.

Of course there are also problems with this kind of cooperation. If you are like me, you like to have control over the whole production including how the script is written and especially over what point of view to take. In this imperfect world, however, I often had to drop that attitude and accept reality. It can lead to some sharp differences of opinion, but it can also lead to a more broadly based production, something less one-sided than what might have emerged if it had been totally in my hands. To meet the needs of a wider audience, giving up a bit of ego is a small price to pay.

We were interested in doing a documentary with our local Historical Preservation Committee whose annual fundraiser was based on public tours of local buildings with historic architectural features. These popular tours led us to wonder if we could put a generic version of them on tape, led by knowlegeable tour guides. It would be performing a bit of historical preservation of our own. Once a tour was past history, many buildings became inaccessible to the public. They changed over time or were demolished, all in the name of progress. Putting them, along with their unique features, on videotape would have been a true public service, and it also met our demand that the subject be of interest to a large segment of our patrons.

Like many historic preservation groups, however, ours was a loosely organized group of individuals whose private scholarship efforts only melded once a year, when they prepared the tours. Getting their permission as a group to film the tour was difficult, and getting them to consider letting us do a private tour (which is probably the only way to get it on tape with any coherence) was even more difficult. They were not putting obstacles in our way as much as they were so amorphous an organization that getting them together was a major hurdle.

From this effort, however, finally came an agreement from them to provide us with a customized tour, one which they would set up by getting permission from owners and also by preparing scripts that called attention to unique architectural aspects of each building. It was even more helpful to have them explain in subtext just where those features were located so that the cameraman would be able to zoom in on the appropriate area as the narrator commented on it.

This is the sort of research that would have taken us much too long to achieve on our own. In fact, I doubt that we would have been able to do even a small portion of the work, since very little written material existed about individual buildings. Even more difficult for laymen to match was the scholarship it took, not to mention the architectural background needed to identify the details that made each building so fascinating.

It was again a problem of timing, since we had to plan our videotape tour when the public tour was over. By the time these experts had set up the information for the basic script and were ready to plan the actual taping, I was deeply involved in the library's fund raising drive and unable to work with them. I can only hope that they will continue their interest in the project and complete it despite my no longer being there to work with them.

I suppose that's a kind of left-handed success, to have what's referred to as viable projects still on the boards when you move on. In the case of the library, there were about a half dozen ideas in various stages of completion, including one on the enlargement of the library's facilities, still pending when I left.

SUMMING IT UP

What this all boils down to is that there are groups of individuals in your own community who will gladly do the legwork for you, put together priceless research, and even use their good offices where needed to get permission to tape people or places when your own efforts might be fruitless.

Look around at these organizations. A lot of them are associated with museums or clubs; they have a kind of bond that can save you days, even weeks, of chasing down leads. Some of the things we had in our hopper included taping memorabilia collected by a local man tracing the history of fire departments in the area; a history of Italian immigrants who came to Racine, planted their tomato and herb gardens, and left a legacy of music, food and raucous good neighborhoods that will make a fabulous story; and a tape of generic legal information for the lay person.

Just running your fingers down the Yellow Pages or checking in your Club File, if your library keeps one, will give you more ideas than you could begin to turn into projects. In every group, every club, there will be a circle of people eager to use their time and talents to help you record significant things about your home town and its history. Enlist their aid, let them do the initial contacts for you, and you'll save an incredible amount of time and frustration.

And one more thing while we're checking those lists. Be sure to find out which corporations or businesses in your area utilize video on a large enough scale to have sophisticated equipment on hand. Be sure to look at schools and hospitals as well. You may be able to enlist the aid of one of their technicians, or, as we were able to do, make some improvement in your product by borrowing technology that you don't have. Special effects machines, character generators with fonts far beyond your wildest dreams, even computer based video technology, might be within your grasp if you ask for it.

The worst thing anyone can say when you ask for their help is no. So make those lists, make a few phone calls, and maybe you'll make some wonderful discoveries about getting talented people to work with you for free.

When you have those wonderful people all lined up, though, you'd better have something for them to work with. That's where script writing comes in. Not only do you have to know how to write scripts for your productions, but you have to know when not to write a script. You have to learn how to be ruthless with the blue editing pencil — especially when those golden words are your own. So in the next chapter we'll talk about blue pencil boldness, and what it takes to come up with a workable script.

FIVE

Blue Pencil Boldness:

What's Good,
What's Bad
and
What's Ugly

IN THE BEGINNING

Behind every good videotape production is the script. Whether it's hewn in stone with every word carefully orchestrated or it consists of a penciled outline on legal paper, you need to have a plan for every tape you produce. Putting that plan on paper makes it a tangible entity; you'd be amazed how many obvious things can be overlooked if you don't go through the whole process on paper first.

There's more than writing a script that goes into the scripting process — as I'll explain in this chapter. But for practical purposes, let's take the whole process apart, put it all together, run it past your talent, and then come up with the written word; I'll show you a partial script and how to lay it out for the actors and the camera operator. First things first: let's get back to our paper plan.

BACKGROUND

Working with factual matter does not let you off the hook. Whether you're dealing with historic facts or demonstrating services, you still need to come up with an interesting storyline divided clearly into a beginning, a middle and an end. You can't leave things dangling, and you can't assume that people will understand your major points without explanation. Everything that legitimately belongs in your production has to be planned for and put into context. You have to play Devil's Advocate and ask all the obvious questions, since your audience certainly will. It helps to break your planning down into discrete segments, and then make sure that each blends cleanly into the next, with no gaping holes in your story.

It also helps at this time to make notes in each segment about how you can demonstrate each point of your story. Should you use an interview? Voice-over footage? Visual elements only? Remember to aim for a good balance of these techniques to make sure you're not producing an alternative to the sleeping pill.

Run three lines across your paper, dividing it evenly into a top section, a middle and a bottom. Your plan will begin right here between these lines as you put in writing just how you want to start, how far you intend to be by the middle, and how the tape will end.

LET'S DEFINE OUR TERMS

On the topmost line of your legal pad (I always worked from a legal pad; it gave me plenty of room) you need to define just what your production is about — in other words, the theme.

Is it a how to? If so, to whom is it directed? Your theme should be something you can summarize very briefly. In fact, if you can boil it down to a few words, you know you have a clear idea of where to go with your production. At best, you'd better not need more than a single line to explain your storyline.

For example, when we did the tape on origami, we knew we had a program about how to fold paper into useful and amusing shapes, and that our audience consisted of middle school children. The theme, then, would have boiled down to: teaching Japanese paperfolding skills to kids.

There were subtexts, of course. Our performer, in addition to knowing how to make these delightful creations, also knew a great deal about the history and background of the art itself, and could relate stories about the ways these objects were used by herself and others in her homeland.

I'm pushing this idea of a theme hard because it was one of the most difficult things I had to learn myself. If you don't immediately define your theme, you can go off chasing your tail — and messing up the structure of your script — following a subtext instead of a theme. A scattershot approach wastes your time and energy and you'll wind up with something that simply doesn't work.

Defining your theme is far more difficult than it might appear at first blush. If you looked at the origami idea and decided that it really was about the history of an art, your whole approach would be shifted; you would pass by the actual process of creating the objects and concentrate, instead, on getting your facts carefully documented. You would brush off any commentary on how contemporary Japanese people make use of origami, for example, and put all your eggs in a historical basket instead.

You might even get into some heavy stuff about how other plastic arts developed in the West concurrent with origami. You could get extremely esoteric about the whole thing and have everyone confused about what it was you were doing. And, if you remember how valuable time is in any of your creations, you'll realize just how unproductive it would be to start researching this theme instead of sticking with what attracted you in the first place.

While the historical aspect of the subject is indeed fascinating, it's not what the children's programs were about. In fact, it would lose most of its fascination for children and skew the target audience about 180°. What had been a sure-fire attraction would become a dust-covered tape box, pulled out only when an art student or fan of Japanese culture wanted some in depth information about how origami began. Any savvy reference librarian can tell you how often that happens.

This paper chase might have happened to us if we hadn't looked at the real theme of our proposed production. Determine what the public's interest in any subject really is before you arbitrarily decide to pull out a single aspect of it and scrap the rest. Yes, people were interested in the way the art developed in Japan, but our performer was doing just fine adding commentary to cover that aspect *while she was explaining how to make origami objects*.

When we made a tape about the city's founder, we again had a theme handed to us; or did we? We had to remember that the sesquicentennial celebration, which had been the reason for the Yorgans' work in the first place, was only a subtext to the production. In this case, we had to keep our eyes firmly on the ball, which was the story of the life of Gilbert Knapp.

While the founding of the city was central to the story, we needed to incorporate everything that Jim and Vi Yorgan had learned about the Captain's life, from the date and place of his birth to the circumstances following his death.

It was interesting to know that the actors had put this performance together in observance of the 150th anniversary of the city's founding, so we kept that fact in mind by doing a "post-Knapp" addendum to the tape in which the actors break character and speak as themselves, telling how they came to impersonate the Knapps. It was of interest to local historians and theater buffs, but it was added after the story was complete so the tape could be stopped before that point if this aspect of the story was irrelevant to a particular audience.

In neither of these cases did we have to create an actual written script. It was enough to go over the basic presentation, consider how best to showcase each aspect of it, and then draw up a shooting schedule. We also had to allow for the fact that our shooting plans included using Historical Museum rooms to showcase the material.

But we also needed to go over the basic story with both actors to avoid a gaping hole in the narrative when we went to put it together. Luckily, we were able to shoot in story order, so that before we shut down for the day and restored those Museum rooms to their former arrangement, we made sure to include everything that required that setting.

It helped a great deal that the Yorgans had made notes for themselves which they consulted to doublecheck their lines. And after seeing the first raw tape we shot, they felt much more confident about how their performances were going. This gave them the impetus to ignore the camera and just tell the story.

ONE, TWO, THREE

In the case of the origami taping, we were able to plan our project by simply asking Keiko to outline which objects she would be demonstrating and then figuring out a timeline for them. Item A would be done first, then Item B, then Item C, and so forth, in a carefully arranged sequence.

Once that was determined, we arranged for an empty meeting room in which to film and borrowed a second camera so that we could cover the demonstration from two perspectives at once. We taped the demonstration in exactly the same way it was performed for school children. In this way, we interrupted Keiko's train of thought as little as possible, reduced down time to an absolute minimum, and used the least amount of her time and ours in the taping of her techniques.

Creating this version required more post-production work than the Knapp tape, however, because Barry came up with an idea that made the demonstration as clear and helpful as possible; he reviewed the various steps as they were demonstrated and then listed the instructions directly on the tape, a painstaking but extremely helpful device that reinforced the visual demonstration.

This is where a character generator can really pay for itself. Without supplemental instructions repeated in this form, the demonstrations would have been much harder to follow. Even people with excellent 4-head players to hold the picture in *pause* with minimal skew would be frustrated trying to follow each step. Besides, you never want to create a program that people will want to leave in the pause mode a lot; it's absolute murder on your tape.

NAME THAT THEME

If you think explaining the theme of a production that you've created is going to be easy, think again. You may well find that you and your team have different concepts of what's to be accomplished, which makes it very difficult to sell an idea to the administration. Defining your theme also forces you to consider the best way to present that theme, since obviously each will differ. Let's take a few more easy examples just to bring the concept home.

When we put together a videotape for a hard-sell package demonstrating the library's need for expansion, we had already amassed a large volume of text and statistical data to substantiate the premise. What our theme boiled down to, essentially, is that the library had a demonstrable problem of overcrowding. Just as they taught you in school, you first need to determine what your real problem is, rather than confusing it with the effects of that problem. Given that understanding, we could move on to illustrate the problem by showing the effects and their link with the cause.

Some of our choices were obvious: we could easily show crowds in the main circulation or stack areas, the overburdened children's room bursting at the seams during story hours, and the lack of seating available for basic studying and reading purposes.

But other things could not be shown that easily. To cover those elements, we decided to incorporate graphics in the form of two charts. One of the charts showed comparisons among five similar Wisconsin library communities in terms of population vs size of library. The other chart showed how easily the main roads in Racine led to the lakefront area where the library was located.

Charts, however, can be just as deadly dull on video as they can be elsewhere. We kept to our main axiom, which was to show rather than tell.

Actually, we did both, using the narrative to point out the facts, and the pictures to illustrate the words. And we had to go beyond our own library to provide the best illustrations possible. We went to the different libraries listed on the chart, and clarified those startling numbers with the even more startling pictures of spacious and beautiful facilities, demonstrating the sharp contrast between them and our cramped, not very aesthetic little building.

We were trying to fill in all three portions of our legal tablet outline. The theme was not just overcrowding. We had to illustrate how inadequate the present building was. We had to *demonstrate* that inadequacy in every way we could. When you do something like this, you also have to consider what questions your statements might raise in a viewer's mind.

In this case we thought about those people who felt a whole new building at a new location (preferably very close to where they lived) would be the most practical solution. There were also people who loved the idea of multiple branches rather than a larger main library. So part of our demonstration required that we show the reasons why these alternatives were rejected.

We listed all the reasons why it made financial sense to enlarge on the present site, and had our narrator discuss these factors while standing near the location chosen as the expansion site. We then listed all the problems encountered in adding branch libraries while standing in front of what was then the only branch in the city. If we had kept to a neutral background or stayed within the main library to cover these points, we would have had our audience nodding off very quickly, long before our 11 minute production had run its course.

While you have to address questions raised by legitimate concerns about your theme, there's no obligation on your part to include every possible nitpicky point dragged in by the querulous. You can see why writing down all of this in a basic outline before writing a script is so important. It's too easy to find you have the whole thing ready to go and then discover something needs to be put in — and you've left yourself no room for it.

That's why you must talk to everyone who has knowledge about what you're trying to do, gathering facts, queries and viewpoints beforehand. Then you take all these things and run them through the template of your theme. If someone felt, for example, that automated circulation was the main purpose of your approach, and if you took this as fact, you could wind up skirting the real issues in pursuit of a subtext. If, on the other hand, you dismissed the whole concept of automated circulation as irrelevant to the overcrowding problem, you've missed a salient point that your critics will be happy to point out to you — later.

A BEGINNING, A MIDDLE AND AN END

Putting central points into the appropriate spaces on your paper will help you think out just which items are important enough to build a segment around, and just how they keep the storyline moving toward the end that you've envisioned. Something that seems to belong near the end might need information added up front to make it intelligible; what you had thought of as a great beginning may turn out to be a trap instead, calling for multiple awkward flashbacks to fill in the background. That's why they invented erasers; it's a lot easier on paper than on tape.

In the process of putting it all together into a script, you need to know what theme to pursue, how best to illustrate it, and how to do all of it in an absolute minimum of time.

Keeping your production relatively short is not just an economy move. In this day of music videos and nanosecond commercials, people have become accustomed to grasping things quickly. The younger they are the less patience they have with long explanations. I won't go into the philosophical aspects of this phenomenon, but consider it a basic rule to follow. Give them everything they need to know, give it to them quickly, as entertainingly as possible, using — forgive me for this bit of newspeak — manageable sound bites.

This approach requires a lot from you. You have to understand what you're doing. I started a lot of projects with a vague approach, but before I could sell the concept, much less produce it, I had to pour concrete over the idea and see what shape it took.

Once you have a theme, you need to think about all the elements that will carry that theme forward. These elements get listed

on your three-section page. If you find yourself getting beyond
your depth as you get into a subject, that's when you look for help.

You must also think about continuity, so the pieces fit together
without leaving your viewer confused about how you got from A
to B. Continuity means many things, including knowing exactly
where everything was when you did a scene, so that the speaker's
attention doesn't move from one subject to another in your completed tape. It means that when you put all the parts together they
make sense. You also need to think in terms of *visual* continuity.
Let me give you a good example of what I mean by that.

The head of our circulation desk once did a tape for us in a plaid
blouse which she enjoyed wearing — at the time. When it turned
out that we needed more footage of her that would blend with the
original tape, she was asked to wear that blouse again; and, as it
turned out, again and again, while the taping ran on for a whole
week. She's not as fond of that blouse now, after washing and
wearing it five days in a row. But in the finished tape, we're the
only ones who can tell which part came first and which was added.

THE STORYBOARD TECHNIQUE

One way to figure out how your plot will work visually is to
use the storyboard technique. A storyboard is exactly like the
cartoon strips you see in newspapers. A series of boxes is your
starting point. Inside those boxes, you outline the major movements that you expect to tape in the process of putting your documentary together.

There's been so much attention paid to this technique, perhaps I
don't have to explain too much about it here. But for those of you
who wonder what I'm talking about, I'll briefly outline the process.

In a series of frames on paper — you can buy storyboard
sheets, sometimes from a source as unexpected as your local university bookstore — you sketch in the basic scenes you envision to
carry your story. You keep to the major changes, i.e., from interiors
to exteriors or long shot to closeup. If you don't use a commercial
storyboard sheet, remember how a television screen delivers the
image. A TV picture is always two parts height to three parts
width, so don't go drawing something taller than it is wide. Your
camera won't oblige you.

If you can sketch even minimally, you can draw out the basic
action of each major point on a storyboard. You can build in visual

variations, long shots vs closeups vs pans, etc., to keep the production from becoming static. A storyboard becomes a visual outline of your shooting schedule and can be an early warning system if what you've been envisioning is not workable.

You could examine some of the better cartoons in your newspaper (I favor *Calvin and Hobbes*, myself) and see how the cartoonist has boiled down certain emotional and attitudinal themes into a bit of exaggerated body language or facial expressions. This is essentially what you're doing in your storyboard. You'll also want to include over-the-shoulder shots, allow for graphics, and in general record everything that will be a significant departure from what has gone before.

You know your plans are not going well when the entire board consists of closeups of talking heads, or long shots of the Rockies.

Early on, during college classes, I took black & white 35mm shots of what I wanted to frame in the video camera, developed that film as contact strips, cut the frames apart, and laid them out in a storyboard format. This is a very sophisticated and time-consuming technique, but it is one sure way to tell if what you are picturing in your head will work in the camera.

Underneath the "frames" on your story board there will be some lines for writing appropriate segments of text, to clearly identify what's going on in each picture. On these lines you can put a bit of dialogue, or add the fact that at this point music will slide in underneath and where it will build to a climax.

When timing your script, you probably will have to read the text out loud to be exact, but a good rule of thumb while you're writing that first draft is *one minute of finished tape to one double-spaced page of dialogue.* Allow exact time for action, of course.

WORKING WITHOUT A NET

If you are fortunate, as we were, you'll have an experienced technician like Barry, capable of running a storyboard right in his head. Given the basic script and an understanding of the purpose of the production, he was able to keep mental track of ins and outs, giving himself plenty of leeway for cover shots just in case.

It wasn't always possible to predict when an interview was going to be tightly edited or allowed to run, but we varied the shots as much as possible to allow for some movement, even when talking heads were all we had to work with. We always thought in terms of "Plan B," that famous alternative to the way it was 'sposed to be, and took extra footage of everything — yes, just in case.

The main purpose of the outline and/or storyboard is simple: you are working in a medium that is visual. You have to learn to think in pictures. You must understand why each scene has to visually relate to the previous one. It's far too easy to gloss over a section of the script if it reads well. It's only later on, when you have to actually put the thing on tape, that you realize there's no way to do it.

If you want a simple example of visual problems, think about the last time you noticed a real *faux pas* in a movie or on television — the hero leaves in a blue shirt and comes back in wearing a red one, or the plants in the background have moved from one side of the set to another when only a second was supposed to have passed.

It isn't often you see mistakes like that in professional productions, because there's someone on the set assigned to cover *continuity*; that detail-oriented piece of business that insures everything is in the right place at the right time, no matter how much later it really is that you pick up a scene to continue shooting.

It's unlikely that you'll have acquired a large enough staff to have a person assigned to such tasks, so you can guess right now who's going to do it. Review your raw tape to make sure that everything is where it ought to be, and all the costumes match. Remember our circulation desk manager and that plaid shirt? It's things like that that keep you from jarring your audience and breaking their concentration on your message. It takes time to check everything out, but lack of observation on your part is no guarantee that your audience will be similarly afflicted.

STARTING THE DRAFT

Once you have your theme set and have decided how you will lay out your shooting schedule, you need to start actually writing the script. The first time you draft it, just get down everything you need as you think of it. Keep your legal pad notes handy so that you don't overlook something you placed carefully in one of those three sections. It may affect the way you expand or shorten each scene. But when you get close to the point of handing this script to someone to perform, you need to take a copy of that script and read it — out loud.

And even after you've read it aloud, changing anything that sounds awkward into simpler, cleaner text, you may find that the person who has to say the lines will have a different speaking pattern from your own. Unless the exact wording is of monumental importance, let them adapt the phrasing to their own style. It will show in the finished product and make you — and them — look very good indeed. Better than if you had insisted on following your script to the letter.

If there's one rule of writing scripts you must remind yourself of constantly, it's this one: don't ever get hung up on your own words. Keep the sentences simple, relatively short, and always conversational. Write the words the way they will be spoken.

This is not an English exam. Dangle a participle if you want to. If you've done all the preliminary work you should have done up to this stage, actual scriptwriting will go fairly fast, provided that you understand one thing. There is no such thing as a finished script. Even though you may have spent months researching your subject, and the phrases you've put into your characters' mouths are perfect, melodious and to the point, you must distance yourself from those words in order to see the project as it is.

Every script we ever used provided us with a foundation — a place to start from. No matter how well you have anticipated all the things that you want to have in the production, something can come up that is so good, so perfect for the work, that it kicks your script right out. If you remain rigid and refuse to recognize luck when you see it, you'll be the poorer for it.

CHEAT SHEETS

You also need to understand that when your narrator speaks on camera using scripted dialogue, you have two alternatives for having that speech go well. Either the person has to memorize the words, or you must come up with idiot cards for him/her to read. Please, please don't ever have them read from the script on camera. Nothing can justify that.

Using cue cards can lead to some very interesting moments. I once put a speech for a library trustee on a series of large posterboards so that she could read them, looking just under the camera to give the appearance of spontaneity. These cards were heavy and awkward to hold, and it took about five of them to hold the full text of a two-minute speech. It was tough going to shuffle them, since I was unable to see the text and had to guess when the next one needed to be lifted into place.

We flubbed the first two tries, and by that time I was losing it. As the cards got heavier and heavier they began to sink lower and lower down. By the time we got it right — or as right as it was going to get — our trustee was practically reading off the floor.

Still, there are ways to do it. Under normal circumstances, using very large print on posterboards is not a bad way to go. Since I have fairly legible printing, it was usually my job to print out the text. In order to make it large enough to read from a reasonable distance, however, anything longer than a paragraph or two required a whole lot of posterboards. We once used a flipchart, holding it close to the side of the camera, which made the performer look like she was not reading at all. We just had to be very careful not to rustle the sheets as they were turned. Anytime such cue cards are held underneath or beside a camera, it's difficult for the audience to tell that the performer's eyes are not looking directly into the camera lens.

Despite the hazards of helping your narrator to remember those lines, it's very difficult for your talent to work strictly off the cuff. When you write that script, it's not a good move to just throw in lines like ... "narrator describes supernova; add fill shots."

Your narrator, if he or she has any sense at all, will leave you standing alone by the camera. Unless this is an interview with Carl Sagan, who knows one heck of a lot more about supernovas than you do, don't expect an actor to fake it. It's not fair. Give them lines to work with. Let them rearrange them, if necessary, but let them know what's going on in the scene.

Let me give you an example from one of our actual scripts, titled, *Service — Public Is Our Middle Name* (okay, so you'll do better when it comes to naming *your* stuff).

Incidentally, when you're typing up scripts — and guess who gets to do that — putting dialogue in capital letters accomplishes two things. It makes it far easier to read for the actor, who will highlight with a bright marker those lines that he/she speaks; and secondly, it helps the cameraman and director pick up on action lines without struggling through a lot of text.

Two narrators - Terry and Lisa - take turns speaking off camera (music up and under pictures)

Terry

SERVICE IS AN IMPORTANT PART OF EACH OF OUR LIVES
HERE IN RACINE. IN FACT, THE QUALITY OF LIFE IS RE-
FLECTED IN THE QUALITY OF THE SERVICES WE TAKE FOR
GRANTED. WE KNOW WHY WE NEED POLICE, FIRE AND
OTHER SERVICES, BUT WHAT DOES THE RACINE PUBLIC
LIBRARY OFFER THAT WE NEED?

Suggested video (I always *suggested* possibilities to Barry, since he
often had his own ideas about how to do things):
Mailman delivering mail.
Clerk helping patron.
Policeman directs traffic.
Reference librarian on phone.
Garbage collection truck.
Patron in stacks.
Teacher in classroom.
Child in story hour.
Fireman in station.
Patron browsing through magazines.
Crossing guard helping children across the street.
Librarian teaching group.
Kringle being handed to bakery customer.
Child quietly reading.
Waitress pouring coffee for smiling customers.

Lisa

MANY IMPORTANT SERVICES THAT WE TAKE FOR
GRANTED ARE WAITING FOR US IN THE LIBRARY.

THE VARIETY OF LIFESTYLES IN OUR CITY IS REFLECTED IN
THE WIDE VARIETY OF SERVICES THAT THE LIBRARY OF-
FERS.

(Suggested video) Patron smiling as she/he checks out materials.
Montage/pan of library collections. Circulation desk activity:
paperbacks, auto manuals, magazines, etc.

RIGHT HERE AT THE CIRCULATION DESK IS WHERE MOST

OF US INTERACT WITH THE LIBRARY, TAKING OUT MATERI-
ALS — BOOKS, RECORDS, COMPACT DISCS, VIDEOTAPES,
MAGAZINES — A HOST OF THINGS THAT MATTER IN OUR
DAILY LIVES, HELPING US TO LEARN, TO ENJOY, AND TO
EXPAND OUR UNDERSTANDING OF THE WORLD AROUND
US.

(Music up and under Terry)
Terry

SOMETIMES WE FORGET ABOUT SERVICES THAT WE OUR-
SELVES DON'T USE VERY OFTEN. BUT THEY'RE THERE WHEN
WE WANT THEM.

(Video- librarian on phone)

I CAN REMEMBER PLAYING CARDS WITH A GROUP OF
FRIENDS ONCE, AND AN AGRUMENT STARTED ABOUT
WHAT YEAR MOHAMMAD ALI FIRST WON THE HEAVY-
WEIGHT CHAMPIONSHIP. WE JUST CALLED THE REFERENCE
DESK, AND THEY SAID . . .

(Librarian looking through book, picks up phone and talks)
Librarian

YES, HERE IT IS. HE FIRST BECAME CHAMPION IN 1964.
(Terry laughs.)
AND I WON MY BET!

Up to this point, we had been using the narrators to carry the
story, and while you never see them, you do see the things they
describe, which is where Barry's ingenuity comes along. He had to
take my suggestions and bring them to life so that as the voices
describe something, an appropriate illustration is coming on screen.

Now, we shift the focus a bit, since straight narratives can become old very, very fast. We've just introduced the reference desk,
and now we want to show that they do more than look up sports
facts for poker players. Having introduced the character of our
librarian as she answered the phone, we have her hang up the
phone and look at a patron walking up to the desk.

(Suggested video: librarian looks up, a little startled, as Large Biker comes up to the desk, accompanied by young boy dressed similarly to him.)

Librarian

CAN I HELP YOU WITH SOMETHING?

Biker

(In a meek voice) YES, I'M LOOKING FOR MOTORCYCLE RE-PAIR MANUALS. (Turns to child standing beside him.) AND WHERE CAN I FIND SOMETHING FOR HIM TO READ? (Video: Librarian smiles and responds. Cut away to others at the desk as Lisa continues narration.)

Just to show that we had a sense of humor about the whole thing, that ominous looking biker was actually our technical services department head, whose beard was let go without trimming for a few weeks just to help us achieve that "natural," menacing look. A couple of bandannas, a dirty sweatshirt, and voila, a star is born. The young boy in a non-speaking role, by the way, was my grandson. He worked cheap. It cost me a meal at McDonalds.

Lisa

THE LIBRARY HAS A LOT OF WAYS TO GIVE YOU WHAT YOU NEED, WHETHER IT'S A SPORTS QUESTION OR INFORMA-TION ON THE STOCK MARKET — OR REPAIR MANUALS FOR MOTORCYCLES AND CARS. A MODERN LIBRARY USES SOME PRETTY SOPHISTICATED SEARCH METHODS TO GIVE YOU THE ANSWER YOU'RE LOOKING FOR.

(Video: database search on computer, ILL books received, system van delivering materials, patron searching through magazines. CU on patron talking to another reference librarian at desk)

Patron

I NEED SOME INFORMATION ON DATA PROCESSING MAN-AGEMENT.

Librarian

DO YOU MEAN MANAGING A DATA PROCESSING DEPART-
MENT?

Patron

YES, THAT'S KIND OF WHAT I'M LOOKING FOR. I'M A DATA
PROCESSOR, BUT I'VE GOT A NEW POSITION WORKING FOR
SOMEONE WHO DOESN'T KNOW ANYTHING ABOUT DATA
PROCESSING. I NEED TO BUILD SOME CREDIBILITY SO HE'LL
TAKE MY SUGGESTIONS SERIOUSLY.

Note, please, that this is a fictionalized version of what happens
at the desk. I asked the librarians to go through a typical query
interview to show how they got a patron to explain what it was
that he/she wanted, and let me tell you, our 11 minutes would
have been used right there.

BREAKING THE RULES

I also broke my own rules at that point and wrote under the
librarian's response: *wing it*. I remember my earlier remark about
not doing that to an actor, but this was the Carl Sagan of libraries: a
librarian. She could come up with 14 sources faster than I could
ever write them down, and it looked a lot more natural for her to
do it exactly the way it's done in real life.

What I did was make notes in the script indicating what sources
the librarian had suggested to me when we talked over the filming
of this bit. That way Barry had some idea of how to set up the
camera, being able to cover all the territory the librarian would
cover in her "search" for information.

It helps not to have to change set ups when your subject is getting into his/her act; you don't want to be any more distracting
than you have to be, and you certainly don't want to derail a train
of thought that's moving along well.

We covered a few more examples of the types of questions referred to the reference desk by a variety of patrons, and then it was
time to introduce the second aspect of our story, service on the two
bookmobiles. The script approached that shift this way:

(Music up after patron asks questions about compact discs. As music fades, we see exterior shots of the Mobile and Bookmobile neighborhoods.)

Terry

NOT EVERYTHING IN THE LIBRARY IS UNDER A SINGLE ROOF. AND SOME OF OUR ROOFS MOVE AROUND. (Music up & bouncy)

(and under)

Lisa

BETWEEN THEM, THE BIG BLUE BOOKMOBILE AND THE BIG RED MOBILE UNIT TRAVEL TO A TOTAL OF FIFTEEN DIFFER-ENT NEIGHBORHOODS, BRINGING OUR SERVICES TO PEOPLE ALL OVER THE CITY.

(Video: interaction of mobile and bookmobile personnel, patrons. Lots of kids and elderly people.)

Terry

MEANWHILE, BACK AT THE MAIN LIBRARY, THERE ARE A LOT MORE NEEDS BEING MET, IN A LOT OF DIFFERENT WAYS . . .

(Video: interior of children's department during story hour; tots checking out books)

Terry

OUR YOUNGEST PATRONS DESERVE UP TO DATE, HIGH QUALITY, WELL ROUNDED RESOURCES AND EFFECTIVE SERVICES RIGHT FROM THE START, BECAUSE THIS IS WHEN CHILDREN START TO DEVELOP AN ENTHUSIASM FOR READ-ING. ONCE THAT HAPPENS, IT BECOMES A LIFE LONG HABIT, USING LIBRARY MATERIALS TO SATISFY INTELLEC-TUAL CURIOSITY, AS WELL AS READING FOR FUN OR TO LEARN MORE ABOUT SPORTS AND HOBBIES AS THEIR

INTERESTS EXPAND.

We followed this intro of the subject by interviewing a teacher who actually uses the facilities. Although I wrote the script with what she told me in mind, she was free to rephrase the actual wording if she wanted. In this case, she opted to go for idiot cards on a flip chart, and this is what she said:

Teacher

I DON'T KNOW WHERE TO START. THERE ARE SO MANY THINGS THAT THE LIBRARY DOES TO HELP CHILDREN AND THE PEOPLE WHO TEACH THEM — (PAUSE) — I GET A LOT OF HELP IN SELECTING BOOKS FOR CLASS USE — AND I ESPECIALLY LIKE THE IDEA OF TEACHER LOANS, TAKING OUT BOOKS FOR 8 WEEKS AT A TIME. AND THE COLLECTIONS ARE GEARED FROM BIRTH THROUGH THE 8TH GRADE SO MATERIALS MEET A LOT OF DIFFERENT INTERESTS AND READING SKILL LEVELS. THE LIBRARY ISN'T AN ACADEMIC LIBRARY, SO THE MATERIALS CHILDREN CHOOSE FROM PROVIDE ENRICHMENT QUITE DIFFERENT FROM THINGS THEY FIND IN THEIR OWN SCHOOL LIBRARIES.

As you may have deduced by now, the points stressed in this monologue were those that the library administration and the teachers themselves considered most important. The interviews then continued with a children's librarian talking about the services from her point of view. She stressed the fact that many adults as well as children could find helpful topics of interest in easy to grasp, basic formats in the children's collections. This was followed by a quick overview of the varied collections, from hardcover baby books to day care provider kits.

Following our original theme, we moved on to the library benefits appreciated by senior citizens, as well as the more broadly-based popular items such as videotapes, government documents, job-oriented materials, and others.

One particularly successful interview melded the actual life experiences of a patron and her child with a message that we wanted to put on this videotape. The following excerpt from the script illustrates how we approached it:

Lisa

IN ANY CASE, A LOVE OF READING IS SOMETHING WE PRO-
MOTE AND ENCOURAGE, BECAUSE IT'S WHAT LIBRARIES
ARE ALL ABOUT.

Patron(Young Mother)

I CAN REMEMBER COMING HERE AS A CHILD. THE EXCITE-
MENT I FELT WHEN THE STORY LADIES WOULD READ TO US
— ALL THOSE WONDERFUL BOOKS! THAT LED ME TO ASK-
ING FOR MY FAVORITE STORY BOOKS FOR BEDTIME READ-
ING. I THINK I WORE OUT ALL THE COPIES OF DR. SEUSS,
AND THEN WHEN I DISCOVERED WINNIE THE POOH — !
NOW I READ THEM TO MY OWN CHILD, AND THEY'RE STILL
JUST AS GREAT AS I REMEMBER.

While she did this scene, the mother held her three-year-old
daughter on her lap, and as they completed the lines, the mother
spontaneously turned to the child and asked if she liked Winnie the
Pooh, too. The child burst into a bright smile and said, "Oh, yes!"
You can't program or anticipate something like that, but when it
happens, it's beautiful.
We continued with the narrators and patrons talking about their
favorite services; we showed wheelchair-bound patrons using the
security gates and visually impaired persons using a print enlarger
and checking out large-print books; we showed investors browsing
through Standard & Poor's, Barron's and the *Wall Street Journal*;
and we showed comic book collectors checking the latest prices in
our catalogs. In other words, we covered the spectrum of those
things most used and appreciated by our public. Then we finished
up with one more interview with a male patron:

Patron

IT'S IMPOSSIBLE TO IMAGINE LIFE WITHOUT THE LIBRARY.
WE USE IT FOR SO MANY THINGS. MY CHILDREN GET MA-
TERIALS TO HELP WITH THEIR HOMEWORK ASSIGNMENTS.
MY WIFE ENJOYS FINDING INFORMATION ON ARTS AND
CRAFTS. I LOOK FOR SPORTS AND BUSINESS MAGAZINES.
BESIDES THAT, WE BOTH FIND A LOT OF HELPFUL INFOR-

MATION HERE TO USE ON THE JOB.

As the patron turns back to the desk, talking to the staff, our narrator comes on again over shots of the community, ending with an aerial shot of the exterior of the library.

Terry

THE LIBRARY MEANS SERVICE FOR EVERYONE. THAT'S WHY OUR MIDDLE NAME IS "PUBLIC." (music up and under credits)

One note as to format: when I wrote my scripts, even when I was dealing with the first draft, I immediately set up a way of including both proposed video and dialogue side by side, so that when Barry got his copy, he could see what I was envisioning for him to shoot every step of the way. This is what it looked like:

SERVICE: PUBLIC IS OUR MIDDLE NAME

SUGGESTED VIDEO	AUDIO
Mailman delivers mail off camera.	Two narrators taking turns
Clerk helping patron Policeman directs traffic. Reference librarian on phone. Etc.	MUSIC UP AND UNDER PICTURES
Waitress pouring coffee.	Terry Service is an important part of each of our lives here in Racine. etc.
Patron smiling.	Many important services, etc.

As you can see, the notations under *suggested video* are intended only to give the camera operator a quick listing strip of possible shots. In a studio, when dealing with more than one camera, it's customary for each technician to tape a copy of this strip to the side of the camera to show instantly which shots the director is calling for over the earphones, since each shot is numbered in studio scripts. Needless to say, you won't have that situation to deal with, at least, not unless you're successful beyond your wildest dreams.

Occasionally I'd have strong feelings about how something should be handled and include more precise recommendations in the strip, such as "closeup" or "wide shot" of the subject. But for the most part, Barry and I would talk over the shots when we got closer to actual shooting so we knew exactly what each of us meant when we outlined a particular shot.

READY FOR MY CLOSEUP, C.B.

Actually, the term *closeup* means a dozen different things to a dozen different people, and here's where using a storyboard or even looking through the viewfinder of the camera can be the best way to clear up any misunderstandings. When push comes to shove, however, I believe that if your technician is at all competent, you can trust those well-trained instincts to choose the shot. After all, you were trusted to come up with a script that would be workable.

You'd better be sure that you've made it workable. Read the dialogue aloud as a matter of course, and do a little visualizing about what you want to see on screen as the words move off the page and into the harsh world of reality. It's amazing how often people doing the writing can get carried away with their prose and ignore the fact that nothing will illustrate these gems.

That happened, as you recall, with the script we wrote with the Sister Cities Committee. Ten minutes of interesting facts about Indian life in Wisconsin out of a total thirty-minute tape was not only excessive, but more than a little daunting to portray. At a cost of thousands, maybe; but never, never, on the cheap. And frankly, it wasn't well thought out either way.

ORAL HISTORY ON TAPE

You're going to run into something a little different when you deal with oral history. The similarities, however, include the fact that you'll still do your planning on paper, and you still have to have a clear, written definition of what you're looking for, just to keep from driving your camera operator crazy.

Oral history interviews fall into four classical types: autobiographical interviews; topical interviews; process interviews; and unstructured narratives.

In the autobiographical interview, you're looking for the story underlying the life of someone or some group in the community. By its very nature, this type of interview covers significant events in a particular lifetime, but the significance can be either personal or global. It generally follows a chronological pattern.

As an example of what I mean by the more personal autobiographical type, one segment of the Black oral history tape we made included the life story of a Black teacher told in chronological order.

We also did global type interviews in which people told us details of their childhoods that were highly individual, yet the events they described could sound a universal chord in others who lived during the same time.

On the other hand, we recorded a verbatim rap session with two street counselors whose dialogue was not about their own lives as much as it was a description of the frustrations felt by a whole generation of people. As far as we were concerned, both this interview and the one previously described were separate parts of a single oral history tape, since our definition of oral history encompassed all four types of interviews.

Topical interviews, on the other hand, deal with single themes or ethnic groups, institutions, or events. Our tape on the Vietnamese fell into this category, since it not only concentrated on a single group, but narrowed that even more by singling out the experiences that these people had known in the process of adapting to a strange culture after the devastation of war.

It's possible to confuse the Vietnamese tape with a process interview, since this type concentrates its attention on changes or developments in a person, place or comparable subject. Still, keep in mind that this is a very malleable medium, and you don't lose points for following a good story instead of an outline.

THE PROCESS OF PROCESS

A better example of process interviewing might be found in our videotape about the building of the marina and festival site. The process of change was examined through interviews with people who were instrumental in guiding that process. Part of the reason that we dwelt on how things had been in the city prior to the project, economically and attitudinally, was to underline the dramatic difference that accompanied the changes in the lakefront. It was not simply an event — the improvement of a piece of real estate — but the act of a city climbing up off its knees and making a new start.

Unstructured narratives, on the other hand, care nothing for chronological or other outlines, but are more in the nature of a conversation, covering random memories as they occur to the speaker. This works well with people who are natural storytellers, whose personality is such that you need no other structure to keep the audience's attention. The only time an interviewer needs to intrude on this narrative is when a natural question occurs that is not addressed, or when the speaker strays from the subject without adding those details that will make it most informative.

The closest we came to this format was in the interview we held with the Black Muslim teacher who began by telling us the events of his childhood, but then deviated into events and feelings of a more contemporary time. The charm and sweetness of the speaker came through loud and clear in this section of the tape, and very little editing was needed.

In a sense, these divisions into interview "type" are a bit like those "body divisions" often seen in fitness magazines, helping you to determine if you're an ectomorph, mesomorph, or whatever, depending on your degree of musculature. Just as a person can be one type above the waist and another below the waist, so can an interview stray from one "pure" type to another without causing anyone major difficulties.

The only reason you need to think about what kind of interview you're planning is to assist you in coming up with an approach. Keep in mind that you may want one thing and find serendipity stepping in to provide you with something different, but far better. In oral history, always go with the real instead of the planned. But for heaven's sake, show up with a plan, even if you wind up scrapping it later on.

Suppose that you were interested in tracing an oral history of an ethnic group in your city. Let's say that group is Italian. You can save yourself a great deal of research time by checking to see what organizations the Italian people in your town have formed on their own. Whether it's the Sons of Italy or the Roma Lodge, you will always find a small handful of people in each of these organizations who have probably done more background searches than you would ever even think of doing.

Contact these groups and talk to the top people. Keep these meetings small, since it's very hard to get clear information from a large number of people at one time. You can always have more than one meeting if there is more than one group involved. You want two things from these people: you want suggestions about who to contact for possible interviews, and you want their good offices to make these contacts.

In the process of finding out who they think will make the best interviews, you'll often find they've already done some previous work of their own, including videotaped interviews with people you might be interested in recording. If they'll let you see these tapes, terrific. It gives you immediate insight into whether or not particular people will provide you with the information you need, and moreover, it lets you see at once how well their stories come across.

THERE'S ALWAYS A CATCH

You see, there's sometimes a major conflict when you set out to record oral histories; the best stories are not always told by the best storytellers. You may be confronted with people who speak hesitantly, or with a weak voice, or who can never seem to get to the point once they begin a story.

This can often be the case with people suffering from the infirmities of age, and the frustrating part is that they often have the best personal memories of events that will fascinate your audience. But whenever you can, try to interview people who are articulate and able to bring their full faculties to the task; no matter how interesting the material, no audience will tolerate too high a level of frustration to gain that information.

Sometimes, though, you have to compromise. We did, when we chose the individuals to interview for the Vietnamese documentary. In that case, many of the people who would have been ideal for our purposes were very reticent about speaking on videotape, some from shyness, some from fear of imagined political repercussions.

We had to be sensitive to that, and not push our project too hard. When we were able to find a core group of people willing to be interviewed, it was clear that some of them spoke English quite well while some of them had pronounced accents that made their speech difficult to follow. Nevertheless, we chose those portions of the interviews that were most dramatic and ignored how badly or well the speaker delivered the lines.

And we found out something else that was interesting. If the speaker was emotionally involved in the telling, and was speaking from the heart, it didn't always matter how clearly the message was given. Listeners suddenly blocked out all difficulties and clearly heard what was being said, since it was on a level that was readily understood. There is something about truth so compelling that we all hear it. Compare it, if you will, to a particularly good piece of poetry from ancient times, filled with archaic symbolism. Despite this, we all understand the message, loud and clear.

TO SUMMARIZE

Beware when choosing people to interview that you're not caught in a powerplay by the people advising you. While that may sound soap opera-ish, let me warn you about the abundance of headaches out there just dying to share the pain with you. Be sure that you pick up on the nuances of each group whose advice you seek, so that you are not playing anybody's game but your own. It's a godsend if you can find someone not directly involved with the production who can give you some advice on where to go for help with your subject matter.

In our case, it helped enormously to have someone on our staff who could warn us against choosing people in the public eye who would be more interested in self-aggrandizement than in carrying the story of the past into the future. Above all, if you are not a member of the ethnic group you're planning to tape, don't make decisions based on your own (unrecognized) stereotypical thinking rather than on reality.

Listen to a lot of people before you start, and then once you start, be willing to hear some criticism of what you're doing with an open mind. In the final analysis, you won't make everyone happy, but if you feel good about what you finally capture on tape, that's the voice you must ultimately obey.

And we've come full circle in this discussion, because you're back with that legal pad on your lap, kicking around some "what if's" with the staff and coming up with an approach that works for you. How much time will you need to devote to research? How much do you already know about your subject? How much help can you call on to get the job done? How much interest is there in the subject? And, once you've decided all that, who will you interview, and what will you ask them?

You need some basic background on each person you will interview, and the amount of work you must do to get this information will have a lot to say about how many people will be on the tape. We started out being very loose. We narrowed down the number of interviews, and their length, as we went along. By we, let's face it, I meant me — Barry always thought my approach was way too loose and unstructured — and he was pleased to see me head in a bit as I realized how much extra work I'd bought myself by being so, um, open to the moment, shall we say.

Still, it's a great temptation to leave everything in, unedited, when the story is flowing and the person being interviewed is fascinating. I had that problem when we interviewed the teacher whose life was a treasure trove of small triumphs and huge, public successes, and while she valued the latter, she took equal pleasure in the former.

Her narrative style was completely natural and warm. Lucid stories burst from her with very little guidance from me. At the request of her clergyman we made a dub of the unedited interview so that it could be used in Sunday School lessons for children at her church, since it was so warm and spontaneous.

The actual interview ran too long to be left intact on our finished tape since the production included three other lengthy interviews. But it was a great story on its own, particularly in the way her church planned to use it. And it was our policy to make copies of unedited interviews for participants who requested them. Heaven knows, it's the only pay they received!

When you have your background questions about potential subjects well in hand, you can start writing out a series of open-ended questions intended to prime the pump, so to speak, and get the subject going in the direction you want. Just beware of asking anything that can be answered with a simple yes or no. Keep those questions open-ended at all times.

Those questions can be as direct as you wish: "How did you happen to become interested in building nuclear devices, Dr. Strangelove?" Or they can be very broad: "Tell me about your childhood, Mr. Capote." Remember that you're dealing in the coin

of goodwill, and while it may be accepted television usage to con-
front interview show guests, you are not Geraldo Rivera. You're the
good guy, remember? Be sure to make that clear to the people in
front of the camera.

DETAILS, DETAILS

If you are dealing with an ethnic group, it pays to have some
questions ready about, for example, the period in which their
families first came to the city, what occupations they pursued, the
numbers of children they had and where those children may have
moved if no longer living in town, what churches, businesses and
clubs they were involved in, and what their feelings are about how
things are currently going for them and their children (that last
alone is good for a couple of hours of heated conversation).

Then you need to have some more personally tailored questions
ready; was the subject part of a locally famous company, musical
group or an artist of note? Narrow in on significant items that will
tell your audience more about these things.

Sometimes there will be stories about events that took place
during an otherwise unremarkable lifetime: did your subject remember the Great Spanish Flu Epidemic after WWI? How was his
family affected by this? How were other families in the area affected? Did these effects include local businesses, or one group
more than another?

You can see how one set of questions can lead naturally to another. Be sure, however, that you keep the subject on track, even
when doing an unstructured interview. Don't let your interviewee
wander up blind passages and lose the point of an anecdote because you want to be polite. Cut in with a question that pulls it
back. You can always edit out your own voice later.

And there's another point. If you don't have someone else doing
the interviews, strive for a tape that gives the impression that your
part of the interview never existed. Plan to edit out those portions
where your voice could be heard, and don't have footage of yourself reacting to those questions, no matter how pertinent you think
it might seem. The subject is the only person who matters on the
tape. The interviewer should, for all intents and purposes, vanish.
Don't do anything to distract the audience from the subject at hand.
The only person I can think of who seems to be able to break that
rule with impunity is Bill Moyers, but the quality of his questions

adds a dimension that overrides the basic rules. Most of us, alas, are not Moyers.

Once you have your raw interviews on tape, you have to face the intimidating task of editing them. If you get as involved in the subjects as I did, it helps a lot to have someone whose approach is more pragmatic, who understands the difference between leaving *everything* on tape — always my first instinct — and narrowing it down into those informative bits that make the story flow and carry it forward.

Luckily for me, that was Barry's approach. Despite the snaps and snarls we exchanged from time to time, I must confess that his impatience with dragged-out segments versus my sense of outrage at cutting things I considered fascinating somehow evened things out.

But knowing up front what effect you want to achieve helps the editing process immeasurably. In our editing of the Black history videotape, we kept an unstructured format approach, editing only for length; even at that, it came in at 100 minutes, a bit unwieldy for all but the most fascinated viewers. Schools preferred showing it in segments, to fit a particular need for information. Still, given the interviews we used, it would have been far more difficult to blue-pencil the work more intensely.

On the other hand, with the Vietnamese tape, we were dealing with a subject that required tight editing, and which fit into our written blueprint perfectly. I still agonized every time we had to choose between one anecdote and another, but in the end, it was the right way to present it, and I knew it.

In retrospect, this was probably one of the most successful productions we did, because it fit perfectly into a tightly regimented format. We did what communications teachers preach from Day One: ". . . tell them what you're going to tell them, then tell them, then tell them what you told them." That's exactly what we did.

We opened up with an introduction by Professor Neuenschwander that placed the work in context, went into each of the segments as outlined, and then finished with a quick overview by the participants. It was classic. And it worked.

This approach would not have been as successful with more open-ended interview tapes, so it's not a template that can be applied to every case. But by this time you've had a chance to think about which of these approaches will work for your particular situation; or perhaps, you're totally open-minded and ready to experiment with them all. Either way, grab your legal pad, try to remember how many people owe you favors, and get going on that production!

You've had a glimpse of the basic skeleton of videotape productions. You should, at least, have a pretty good idea of the kind of preliminary brainstorming you need to do in order to come up with a basic theme, a list of participants, the type of cover footage you'll need to illustrate your story, and a basic timeline of how you're going to do the actual taping.

Part of the basic planning you will be doing is setting up appropriate places to shoot your material. When doing interviews, it's usually best to tape in an environment that is comfortable for your subject. Sometimes that turns out to be the person's office, or home; sometimes it might be more comfortable to shoot in your own office or meeting room; and sometimes, the storyline dictates the location.

An example of that last situation would be the tape about the harbor project, where the site itself was the story, and therefore, all interviews or narrative elements that could be done on that site were planned that way.

Common sense tells you that you want to have a background that fits the mood and purpose of the tape. Interviews with people for oral history purposes are usually done in their own homes, to help them relax, and also to surround them with familiar things that lend another aspect to the tape. People's homes are often extensions of their personalities, and this adds credibility and interest to the interview.

On the other hand, most interviews tend to concentrate photographically on the upper body and the face of the person speaking, and little is seen of the background unless the cameraperson makes a special effort to broaden the range of some shots to take in the surroundings.

All of these uses depend on two factors: you have to have permission to shoot anywhere outside of your own facility, and your subject has to be comfortable with the site chosen. That's something you take care of in a site survey, and that's just one of the subjects that's covered in the following chapter.

Coming up next, you're going to take all the things you've learned up to this point, and you're going to put it all together to create a videotape that will be the best you can make it.

SIX

Putting It Together:

How To Make All Those Pieces Fit

OUTTA SITE

If you've come this far, you've put a lot of preparation and planning behind you. You have the world's best script, a lineup of free talent that would turn Spielberg green, and shiny new equipment that's just champing at the bit to be put to work. What now?

Pick up that legal pad, the one I know you're never without since starting to think about doing your own project. It's time to set up a planning sheet, and a large part of that sheet will be taken up by an extensive checklist. If you think you did a lot of planning when you wrote the script, consider that good practice for what you're going to do now. Take out your notes and check out your storyboard.

This is the time to think it all out. What do you need to complete this particular taping project? If you have your theme set, and you know who your talent will be, your next decision is where you'll be doing your taping. The theme, of course, dictates to a large extent the location or locations of your shoot. Unless you have a wonderful studio out of which you never plan to move, you need to know just what you're getting into when you step out that door with video equipment in hand. What *might* you need, in terms of materials, blank tape, equipment, personnel and travel facilities in order to do everything you have planned?

An important activity right at the start involves setting up a "survival kit" in which you store extra cables, tape, batteries, and adaptors. We used a large canvas library bag, but almost anything that can bear the weight will work. Never assume everything will go right when you're on a shoot. In fact, the second basic theorem of videotaping consists of two parallel facts: *Every day something breaks. Everything that breaks is critical.*

So you need to have a very good idea of what you're getting into, both literally and figuratively, when you set up your shoot. In other words, you're going to do a site check. While it's not always possible to pay an advance visit to every place you plan to use as a location, do check it out in person whenever you can, and do it thoroughly, with your checklist in hand. If you absolutely can't get there ahead of time, do a phone check. You'll save yourself a lot of frustration if you call beforehand and ask the right questions.

YES, ANOTHER LIST

Make sure the person you're talking to has the knowledge to answer your questions. Who that person is will differ every time. Sometimes it will be a custodian, sometimes the chairperson of the board. Never take "I think so," for an answer. The questions from your checklist will include:

- the name of a person on site you can use as a reference/ resource/helper
- information about the size of rooms for interior shooting
- the number of outlets on each wall for plugging in equipment
- where the circuit breakers are located
- if it's to be an exterior shoot, availability and location of power outlets
- will the area you're working in be open to the public while you're shooting?
- and above all, what conditions will you find in terms of light and sound — wall-size windows? no windows at all? noisy air conditioners? onsite mikes? is this part of a larger room with a divider? what else is going on in that area?

When you can do an in-person site check, there's a great deal more you can learn just by looking at the actual conditions under which you'll be working. By walking around the area, you can experience first hand any conflicts between the needs of your script and the realities of the location. You can tie specific scenes into specific areas. You're looking for several things; you want to know your lighting conditions, you want to recognize your sound constraints, and you want to get the general lay of the land.

In-person site surveys allow you to "play camera" by holding your hands in the shape of a frame before your face to block in how much or how little of the background will show up in your widest shots. You can look at colors and details of furniture and decoration. The placement and quantity of these items will determine how crowded your taping area will be. Check on how much maneuvering room you'll have. How much can you move out of the way, and how much must you work around?

You can literally walk through your script and consider what clothing colors will work best for your performers, for example, or what to avoid at all costs (like white shirts, especially with dark complexions). Take notes as you go along, because your memory may or may not hold true, especially if there is more than a day between the site check and the shoot.

A LITTLE LIGHT ON THE SUBJECT

Let's start with the lighting situation. You want to know, whether it's an interior or exterior shoot, if you'll need supplemental lights. I'll never forget the day I was sent to tape a conference and had brought no lights with me. The room was held in a dark hotel basement conference room with about as much artificial light as a pair of candles might provide. Needless to say, even if I had brought along all three of the lights, they would have been inadequate for that whole room.

If you decide that you need lights, and that the lights you have will be adequate for the job, is there a source of power readily at hand? Make sure that you look for all the outlets in a room. The more you can spread out the load, the less likely you are to need that information about circuit breakers.

Video is a medium of limited contrast. Film can provide a broad array of shades from white to black, making low light images far easier to see than they would be in the more limited video medium. Adjustment is not easy, and it's important to use your auxiliary lamps to make the light level of interior shots identical to any shot outside. You'll want to have the capacity, in terms of tape and battery power, to make a lot of just in case shots — cutaways, background, something to cover your jump cuts, and so on.

Even when you have adequate battery power, it pays to be able to plug in your recorder and camera to avoid running out of juice for those shots that can only be done on batteries. I can count on the fingers of one hand those times when cold weather or badly charged batteries left us without a way to record what we set out to do. But even once is once too many. Check those outlets.

And as a corollary to that, make your contact person a custodian or someone on site who can help you to avoid overloading the available power source. Usually, if you've looked carefully enough around, you can find enough outlets to let you spread out the load, but it doesn't hurt to have another opinion on what those outlets can handle. It's also helpful if you turn on your lights only when absolutely needed, and let them remain off during setups or any other time you're not shooting.

Be sure to check the type of outlets you're dealing with as well. While most modern buildings have adequate outlets and power to handle your needs, shooting in older buildings can present problems. Video equipment, especially supplemental lighting kits, are all equipped with three-prong plugs for safe grounding. If you have to work with outlets that don't accommodate a three-prong plug, then you need to bring along adaptors, and you must be doubly careful about overload. We always carried at least one adaptor in our emergency kit for just such situations, as well as a second adaptor which was always mounted on our heavy duty extension cord.

Assuming that you're working in an interior location, look around to verify the source of light for the room you'll be working in. It's rare that you find a room that doesn't include mixed sources, that is, part of the light coming from windows and part of the light from a variety of lamps.

If you find that you have inadequate light, or that you will have to shoot directly into natural light streaming from a window, remember that videotape is just another form of photography which depends on light to record material. Set up supplemental lights, carefully define the area in which you will work and towards which you'll direct the camera, and whenever possible when working under your own lights, try to cut off as much outside light as you can.

Pull drapes, or turn your back to the windows — whatever — find some method of controlling the light that enters your camera. If you can take practice footage of the area to be absolutely sure how colors and objects are recording, so much the better. That could be a good time to experiment with the filters built into your camera, or any additional filters you may choose to try.

You may also want to invest in gels for your light kit; blue can balance the light when there's a lot of outside light from windows where you'll be shooting. To match indoor scenes against outdoor footage, you might want to use a yellow gel. These gels are available from photo and video stores as well as lighting equipment stores, and the people who sell them can give you additional information on how to use them for best effect.

Often, shadows provide a source of depth and three-dimensionality to your scene, so you don't want to make your lighting flat to destroy that effect. But often these shadows can be distracting, as well. The best way to eliminate shadows that you don't want is by moving your lights, rather than adding more light. Try to avoid making people look as if they were cardboard figures shot against a cardboard wall.

MORE HANDY TOOLS TO CARRY

For an exterior shot near traffic areas, it helps to set up those orange cones used by the traffic department near your truck or car, and even to use highly visible cardboard signs saying "Video Production in Progress." We stocked the cones ourselves, thanks to our friends in the department of public works, but in fact hardly ever had to use them. Nevertheless, an ounce of prevention is worth hauling those cones with you when you have to shoot in an area where traffic could present a problem.

Another important tool to carry along with you everywhere is *gaffer's tape*, which is a slightly more expensive version of duct tape. You can use this tape to hold your cables down in place and prevent people passing by from tripping over them and a) killing themselves or b) pulling the equipment down and smashing it. Neither of these seems like a good alternative, so take the tape along and use it.

When we did shoots inside Johnson's Golden Rondelle we used a corner of the structure on one side of the seating area that was perfect for setting up the camera and recorder, but the power source lay across an aisle through which people moved with irritating regularity. By using gaffer's tape we were able to fasten down the cables leading from our corner to the plug across the way without causing harm to either the people or the equipment. And it came up easily when it was time to strike the set.

LISTEN CAREFULLY

Check your site for sound distractions. Sometimes the hum of an air conditioner can intrude on a taping, leaving a barely perceptible noise as background sound. You may not even be aware of it until you edit the tape with other footage and discover how intrusive the noise can be. Watch for places that have radio or television transmitters, sometimes housed atop a building you're shooting in or even nearby, and be aware that anyplace with lots of VTDs — computer or video screens — can cause interference in your productions, leaving patterns on your tape that won't go away.

If you're shooting in an area where large equipment is in use, you may also have to change your plans, unless that equipment is part of your story and will provide you with useful ambient sound.

We once had a perfect vista from which to shoot, and our narrator was all lined up in the bright, perfect sunshine — and then a bulldozer began growling at the earth directly across from us, wiping out all possibility of shooting at that time and place. The best laid plans, and all that. You can't always anticipate something like that happening to you; that's when you'll develop your own Plan Bs. When you're doing a site check, make it part of your plan to envision possible alternatives to your first choices.

Is there another room, another building, or the possibility of moving either inside or outside, so that you can use the same time and location despite sound problems? If you were planning to do simple background shots, of course, sound is irrelevant. But if you have people on camera, you want to be able to hear them, loud and clear.

You can usually count on wind screens to handle a lot of natural sounds caused by wind, but it helps to check by using those earphones you're never without.

While it's seldom a problem, keep in mind that your cables, if unshielded, could pick up RF signals, or even cause a hum on your tape if you cross a power cable. Don't put your cables parallel to power cables, but instead set them at right angles to them to avoid interference in a long cable setup. Many minor background sound problems can be overcome with the use of lavaliere mikes and a sound mixer. When we shot the Chiwaukee Prairie footage outdoors at UW-Parkside, the sound of wind in the trees and bushes was quite loud, but our mikes were able to ignore all but the sound of our speakers' voices.

I was astounded when I listened to those tapes for the first time, seeing the wild movement of foliage all around the people on camera. It really helps if you can do test taping for both sound and color to judge actual conditions, but remember that conditions can change unexpectedly. If you're desperate and must use tape with background noise on it, sometimes laying in a bit of music will mask the noise in the editing process.

In cases where a site check can't be done ahead of time, you can still take a careful look around when you arrive and determine what will work and what won't. Let me walk you through the way we did an actual site-check in the process of shooting a program.

LET'S TAKE A LITTLE WALK

When we made the research videotape at Washington Park High School, we were dealing with a classroom setting as well as a library setting. By going into these rooms and looking for the best vantage points from which to shoot, we also discovered ways to improve our plans.

For example, when we went into the classroom, we found that the blackboard was in a perfect light position to be used as an introductory device. We set up the shot from the back of the room. Our teacher, who was exceptionally cool and composed while these crazy AV people wandered through her domain, was more than happy to help us out by writing, in a crisp, clean handwriting, the title of our fictitious subject; this allowed Barry to start the program with a closeup of the blackboard.

As the words were completed, the camera pulled back to reveal a long shot of the teacher "dismissing" the class for the day. This broad shot then expanded even more to show the students rushing into the aisles as they cleared the room. The camera angle, which was behind the students and fairly low, gave the viewer a sense of participation as the students surged out of their seats and towards the front of the classroom.

After that beginning, we moved closer to the front of the room and reshot the same exodus, this time zeroing in on our two "stars" as they moved with the crowd, then stopped near the teacher's desk to begin their dialogue.

A third setup, this time from the other side of the room, allowed us to show the conversation from another angle. This provided us with closeups of the main characters and added movement to what might have been a static scene. Then we zoomed to follow the students as they left the room, walking into the corridor as they headed for the library.

The lighting situation, by the way, was fairly simple, since all the light in the classroom was artificial and very bright. Adjusting the filters took care of color balancing to match the rest of the tape, which was completed with interior shots except for two minor scenes.

It was not necessary for us to show the students walking down the hall towards the library; their destination was implied in the dialogue. But on the principle of Plan B, we did some shots in the halls anyway. Those shots remained on the cutting room floor in the end. But it was a lot simpler to take those shots and find we didn't need them than to have skipped over them in the pursuit of speed and then discover we were in desperate need of shots we didn't have and could no longer get.

To carry our story forward, we could have shown the students entering the hallway and moving toward the library, but we found that we got the same effect by setting up inside the library about 20 feet from the front doors and shooting their entrance through the glass, which saved us one setup and a few seconds of irrelevant nonstory action. Our shooting angle showed them clearly coming towards the doors, going through the glass doors, passing the security gates, and moving directly to the next setup, which was by the card catalogs. And all of this in one setup, using reverse zoom to follow the action.

That set us up for the next sequence, which was to follow the students while they did their own research. Only after that would we move our setup to show them going to the librarian for further help. While the actors mulled their lines, we checked out the library for this part of the shoot.

Barry and I wandered all over the place, having set up the position from which we'd tape the encounter with the librarian. We walked through, looking for camera angles that would tell the story of the students' independent research quickly and without the need for words. By shooting from the stairway, for instance, we were able to show the girl student going to the periodicals desk and looking through them. A closeup, over the shoulder shot of the boy student had him going through various reference sources in the lower stacks. We also took some shots at an upstairs desk just to add a bit of variety to the viewing and to illustrate the number of possibilities available. All of these shots were done without sound, so we were much more mobile than we would have been had dialogue been involved.

By taking only the camera and the recorder, we were able to make up interesting camera angles and vary the work with closeups and wide shots, pans and zooms, giving an impression of swift movement and hectic pace. In one brief scene, we piled up a stack of reference works and shot directly from above, using the architecture of the library itself as inspiration for the best places to shoot.

It also helped that the library was brightly lit, with only peripheral interference from outside window sources. We could use available light to make our task of moving the camera and recorder around much faster and easier. In fact, as we discovered a new angle, we called the kids over and shot it at once. It was a wildly free, open way to work, and we managed to capture the impression that it was all spontaneous action. Probably because most of it was!

That was a case of being more lucky than smart, because things could have been very different in terms of light source and setting. But we had taken our faithful lighting kit along, just in case, and would have been able to adapt to a number of variables. Sometimes, as you will see, you just get lucky.

We had originally given the students the fictitious task of searching for information on public parklands. It was purposely chosen to reflect a topic that would have very little information available through the school library. By the time we had moved the students through the stacks, the reference materials and the periodicals, we had taken up very little time in the tape, but we had shown the natural progression that students would have followed on their own before seeking professional assistance. And, true to our premise, they found very little in the school library to flesh out the topic.

When the students turned at last to the school librarian, we decided to take ourselves a little out of the realm of pure fact and add a bit of fancy. Instead of using straight dialogue, the librarian responded to the kids' request for help by silently handing them a large manila envelope. The twinkle in her eye was evident as they turned the envelope upside down and tapes and clippings fell out, on top of which was a flyer that said, in very large type, **Racine Public Library**. You could almost see a tall, white-haired man smiling tightly in the background as they looked at each other in stunned amazement. Was this mission really impossible?

We had some interesting problems while filming that segment, which I'll describe later on. But I want to digress for just a bit, to show some of the thinking that went into the scripting of this segment.

AND NOW FOR SOMETHING COMPLETELY DIFFERENT

We planned to insert a few bars of the *Mission Impossible* theme to underline the byplay and help the viewers pick up on the whimsy. To our delight, the students were quicker to pick it up than the teachers when the film was shown to them. This was done the year before the program itself made a brief return to the screen.

This piece of business also set the tone for the rest of the tape, so that we could show our dogged, determined students relentlessly pursuing what seemed like an "impossible" mission, finding all the sources for information on public parks.

You can't always take as light an approach as this, but in an instructional videotape, if you can avoid a preachy approach and bring in some aspect of fun, it really helps. People seem to learn more when they're laughing than when they're merely enduring a recital of facts.

Thus far we had spent one day at the school, performing an instant site analysis and moving immediately to shoot the scenes described above. Our plan was to then move on to our own library for the next day's shots. But first we had to sit down for a few moments and review the script carefully, to be sure that we'd gotten everything in. We were not a sophisticated enough production crew to use shot sheets, but it occurred to us that they would have come in very handy at that moment.

SHOT SHEETS AND FIELD FOOTAGE LOGS

Shot sheets are very useful to have, but it's important that you have sufficient staff to use them properly. Most shot sheets are simply a list of shots tallied on a form. They include the program title; notation on whether these are listings made during a shoot or during the editing process; tape number, if you're smart enough to mark your tapes as you go; scene number and "take" number if it's a complex piece of work and you've numbered each of these elements; starting and ending point of each take; and any notes pertinent to the work.

In the best of all possible worlds, these sheets will be filled out as you shoot, so that you know on tape number 3, for example, you have two crowd shots of the classroom; you did four takes before you were satisfied, and will briefly review the first three to see if they were as bad as they seemed to be at the time; each shot started at a certain point in the script and ended at a certain point. By using these shot sheets, you save a lot of editing time later on, and you also check completed shots against the script to make sure that you haven't left out anything.

Another standard form is called a Field Footage Log, which again lists scenes completed during an outside shoot. It's a more down-and-dirty way to keep track of what was shot on any given day.

This is the way it's supposed to be done, and the way that studio professionals work. It's not necessarily the way you'll work, because, first of all, your staff is probably too small to spare a single person to do nothing but keep track of your shots, and secondly, you'll probably be marking your script as you go along to keep track of the shooting.

A quick scribbled list on the stickon label of your tape is probably as close as you're going to get to this elegant technique. You may wind up reviewing more footage than you really wanted to each time you edit, but you'll also have a limited number of tapes to work with on any given production. Your memory, and the notes that you make on the script, will usually be your guides. Sometimes something as simple as a highlighter drawn through a scene will be enough to indicate that the shot was completed.

Keep in mind, too, that while you're shooting these scenes, details are all important. If you show closeups of people supposedly talking to each other, make sure that they are looking toward each other regardless of whether or not the other person is on camera. If you start out with the boy standing to the left and you pull in for a closeup of the girl, be sure that she's looking to the left throughout the scene. If he's shown looking to his left, too, people will be confused about who's standing where.

Watch those details in other ways. In the shot of the students talking to the school librarian, we wound up cutting out a small segment because the girl had moved the strap of her purse from one shoulder to the other between shots of the same scene, and it was impossible to put them together. There's that old continuity problem again. When you're shooting very fast, it can be a trial to keep track of such things, but they really do matter.

When you write the script, think about all the things that don't have to be seen by an audience to be understood. When we were working on this tape, we gave a lot of thought to how the kids would arrive at the library — car? bus? dropped from a plane? Every possibility would require a different setup and approach for shooting and, most importantly, would eat up precious action time.

DOES IT REALLY MATTER?

Then, of course, the obvious hit us: it didn't matter *how* they got there. The only thing we had to show is that they did arrive. We placed our camera inside the main library at much the same angle that we shot the school library entrance, and we had them walk right in and head for the card catalogs.

This day's shoot promised to be a bit easier than the previous day, since we were totally familiar with the library's lighting and power sources, and could move from setup to setup with barely a word to acknowledge what needed to be done. Our attention could be focused completely on what our young actors and their librarian assistants were doing.

From the initial setup we moved to one side of the reference desk to capture several shot sequences. We had two more setups at the main adult level, including shots of the students sorting out an enormous pile of reference material, all of it absolutely authentic. We also did some quick shots with minimal dialogue in the Children's Department downstairs with one student, and then we filmed the students in the process of moving out of the main building, even though the script called for other scenes to be inserted before the ones we were shooting. We wanted to get everything in this setting done while we were there. Whenever you can, it's much more efficient and time saving to shoot everything that's set in one location before moving to another, despite what may be called for in the script. Putting it in correct sequence is what editing is for.

Now it was time to get some footage across the street in the AV offices. We wanted to show one student searching for pertinent films and videotapes in that office, and incidentally learning the difference in research methods between AV and print materials. It was a one-setup bit of business, with the camera set behind the counter and working over the shoulder from the clerk to the student. The scene called for the student to walk in, ask his question, receive information, page through the catalog and — cut. Nothing fancy.

After shooting the scene, we simply brought our camera outside the AV offices and set up for taping both kids, laden with books and other materials, as they walked out of the main library across the street and into the sunshine. At that point, they could have chosen any form of transportation, including helicopter; it didn't matter. We'd made our point without any extraneous scenes being included.

We chose to shoot the final scene of the students leaving the library from the AV office for two reasons: the first, of course, is that we were already there. We'd finished up all interior shots of the main building, and we needed only one last exterior to wrap the shoot. Secondly, the AV office had a raised area in front of it from which we could get an interesting and unusual angle of the kids leaving the front door of the library and heading on "home."

From that angle it would be possible to zoom in on them at the start and then gradually have the zoom fade as they moved out of the frame. We set up, sent the kids to fill their arms with books, and in a moment we were ready to go. The shot, because it was an exterior one, required the use of batteries; but since we had been using inside power through all the other shots, we had more than enough battery power to complete the final shots, even if we needed several takes. As it was, it went quickly. But as a precaution we took the time to run inside the AV office to make sure the color worked well with the interior shots before we let the kids go. Since they were planning to leave on vacation the next day, it was a wise, if unneeded, precaution.

Whether your site check is done ahead of time or on the run, take the time to think about each shot you'll be doing. Consider background, echoes, people walking through, and all those other things that you can miss in the tunnel vision that occurs when you concentrate on what you see in the viewfinder. Take the time to make notes as you go along, no matter how desperate your hurry. Otherwise, you'll wind up looking at a lot of tape that you don't have time to watch, just to see if you did or did not get a crucial piece of information.

Now, let's skip ahead and see what happens when we arrive, bloody but unbowed, with raw tape that we will now turn into a glorious example of videotaped perfection.

VIDEO, MY SUITE

Moving into the editing suite, we have to do two things before anything else: make a strong pot of coffee, and pull out the shreds of your script. Get a fresh copy of that script and put it beside the editing controller.

Making a master tape requires that you follow your much altered script exactly, adding only title footage and ending credits. You've got a pretty good idea of how long the tape will last, but it won't be completely correct until you've actually finished the entire production.

How much time you allow for program length, unless it's intended for broadcast purposes, can be pretty much decided by the needs of the potential user. Generally, we tried to come up with productions that ran from 10 to 45 minutes, since that seems to be the optimum time for a given audience to sit through them. Few ran shorter, but some of our oral histories ran considerably longer. Keep in mind, however, that each segment of those histories was designed to stand alone as well as to be viewed as part of the whole.

If you're planning to use other facilities to do your title, you must have that footage in hand now. It will literally be the first thing on your master, unless you intend to precede your title with a short introductory segment. For the most part, we used our own character generator to put in opening titles, but in some more elaborate productions, we took some footage (or borrowed some appropriate tape) to have the titles superimposed for us. You need to have a piece of tape that works well underneath these titles, not so important that it will infuriate people not to be able to see it clearly because the title obscured it, and not so bland that it seems to have nothing to do with the subject at hand.

After that, you follow the script, laying down your narrative and the scenes exactly as they were planned. This can be the moment of truth. This is when you discover that you have some off camera narration and not a darned thing to put over it. Or you have some fabulous footage that doesn't belong anywhere. But if all went well, this is when you put all the words and pictures together to bring the cold pages of that much-mangled script to life.

Usually it's a good idea to do all the insert editing as you go along, but there's no reason why you can't just lay down the spine of the production and then go back and put in your inserts. Most of the time, however, Barry and I completed each segment before moving on to the next.

This does two things: it gets that segment out of your hair once and for all; and it makes you sick and tired of looking at it and eager to move on to the next portion.

REALITY — WHAT A CONCEPT

Actually, you'll probably experience the same effect we did when working on each segment. You tend to develop a rhythm as you work on each part of the tape so that you instinctively know how much time to allow for each bit of cover you use. When you considered a scene, for instance, you might have envisioned a three second bit of cover at a particular point in the narrative; but when you see it before you it becomes obvious that it needs something more. You'll know, for example, that it needs as much as three three-second segments of cover, each of them brief but pertinent to carrying the story along.

Go with your instincts at times like this. The more you do it, the more you can trust what your feelings are telling you.

Let's continue to use the research tape as our template for the way the editing process works. We opened on the shot of the teacher's hand just finishing the title. There was no sound until the school bell rang out (no, it wasn't a happy coincidence; we taped it while we were there and then edited in the sound at the exact moment we needed it). The teacher called out the homework assignment to underline it for us as the bell faded. We let the tape run for a few seconds as the students rose and trooped brightly down the aisles; then we cut quickly to the second shot of the same students moving toward the camera, leading to the scene where our two actors paused by the teacher's desk. Because we had taped it carefully, we needed little more than basic assemble editing at this point, just choosing our cutting points precisely to keep the action flowing but comprehensible.

We cut again to the two-shot of the students leaving the class-room and heading for the library, at which point we threw in some traveling music and brought up the title of the program on our character generator. That gave us a little continuity as the music came down under the scene of the kids walking into the school library; we didn't cut the music until their first lines were spoken. Then we brought the music up again as we cut in multiple shots of them going through the process of searching for information. It came down again under the scene of the students walking up to the librarian and asking for help.

Music, incidentally, is an ideal way to provide a sense of movement when there is no dialogue and the action is less than intense. By bringing it in, raising the sound and then lowering it when the next scene is about to begin, we cue our viewers into what's happening, and we give them a signal that something else is about to happen as well. For a great example of how this can be used, watch soap operas as they end and begin their sequences. They know as much about that specialized technique as did the old time organ players in the days of silent films. Try not to pick up any of their other techniques, though, especially in scripting.

CONFUSION REIGNS

We found the going a little more complicated when our students moved to the librarian's desk. We had to combine shots of the students coming toward the desk, shot from behind the desk, with other shots of them taped over the shoulder of the librarian. We needed some shots to cover the dialogue from the students' point of view, looking at the librarian's face and expressions. Then we moved the camera to the other side of the desk and shot the librarian's reactions to their questions. And, finally, we had to do closeups of the envelope being handed over, being opened and having the contents spilled out onto the desk.

We had to move camera, recorder and microphones from one side of the librarian's desk to the other while filming these shots, and it began to get a little confusing. Had we gotten each bit of dialogue in before we moved the setup? Had we anticipated reaction shots? Had we kept the tone of the dialogue correct even when shooting out of sequence?

Because each of these shots had a separate setup and was not following the script verbatim, we had to wade through the raw tape in the process of editing to find the optimum point in each acceptable segment that would blend with the previous footage. This is time-consuming, and it's very critical to get it right. A beat too fast or too slow could skew the tape and produce an irritating "off" feeling for us and for our audience.

How do you know when a beat is off? I wish I could give you an exact formula so that you could tell automatically by running it through a calculator. But this is where science bows to art. All I can tell you is that you'll know it when you see it. Unfortunately, you may have to get all the way through and then see the tape as a unit before you recognize it. But you'll only make that mistake once, I assure you. The only cure is to recut that segment, and that's one heck of a lot of work. There are techniques that use music to adjust the balance, but the ideal, of course, is not to be off in the first place.

Editing is the most crucial and nerve-wracking part of the whole production process. It's also that part that's going to give you the most satisfaction if you've done it well. In dealing with the segment described above, for example, we could have simply shot the segment on interaction between the students and the librarian from one point of view, cut it into the narrative and moved on to the next part.

But frankly, it would have put most of our audience into a restless, bored state. Cutting from one viewpoint to another, showing shots of people listening and reacting to each other, gave pace and movement to a scene that didn't have a whole lot of excitement going for it. When you have to do exposition and there's no other way to do it except by dialogue, keep your visual feet moving fast. Jump from one person to another, one viewpoint to another, using jump shots, cutaways and different angles to make it look like something is actually going on.

LISTEN CAREFULLY

When you check each segment as it's completed, in addition to looking at such things as how well the color works for you, or watching for visual balance and making sure that the whole story is being told, you need to listen to how the tape sounds. This is, again, a subjective skill, requiring that the person or persons responsible for producing the tape be the one to make the final decision. It's definitely not something to hand to a committee, unless you're fond of raising camels on your horse ranch.

If something's off and you can't quite tell what it is, try music to change the pace. I mentioned earlier that music can work wonders to create "movement" in something not intrinsically exciting. Note how quickly or slowly a portion of the tape is moving and try playing some background music paced just a hair quicker or slower than the segment moves.

It may be that someone is speaking at a rate that's not quite as fast as other people on the tape. In itself, this is not a problem. But if the segment becomes dragged down by this, or if the tone is somewhat flat, you may find that a light dusting of background sound can pick up the pace, add a bit of flavor to the tone, and generally make the audience perk up its collective ears.

The use of music in video productions is a touchy subject. For the most part, music is protected by copyright and cannot be used in full, or even in large part, without permission of the copyright owner. That permission often comes with a high price tag. And as we all know, libraries have little extra money to pay royalties. Your choices might seem slim, but in fact, they are not.

You might be able to use stock music from local television or radio stations, with their permission. There are types of process music that can be purchased, granting perpetual use rights. You'll recognize a lot of it in the background of local cable advertisements. This is something you have to look into on a case by case basis. If it's worth it to you to have music and sound effects without fear of using them freely, then by all means look into purchasing these tapes or records.

You could also use recordings of music in public domain, usually classics. And, thanks to a quirk in the law, you might just be able to use something more contemporary, as long as you don't use very much of it. You can actually use up to a minute and a half of copyrighted material at one time, whether they're visual or sound recordings, without violating copyright law. If you are planning to produce videotapes for sale or profit, however, it would be a good idea to seek legal counsel before using anything protected by copyright. The kinds of things that we produced were offered free of charge to patrons, even teachers and pupils. No fee of any sort was ever charged, nor were the tapes sold to anyone.

Whichever of these paths you choose to take, keep in mind that music does a lot more than introduce your material and make a nice background for your crawl at the end.

Music, as filmmakers have known for over 70 years, helps to set the scene; it tells you when the excitement is beginning; it tells you when the story is just about over; and it gets your adrenaline flowing when the credits come on and the producer/editor/technician want you to notice the names on the screen.

Music helps set the tone and pace of a production as well. As I said, if you want to give a sense of fast-paced excitement to a some-what slower segment, fast-paced music in the background can do it for you. Alternatively, if you wish to convey an emotion in a scene that has no flavor of its own, music can convey the exact emotion you wish to project. For examples of that, just watch a tape of *The Big Chill*, and see why it created masses of copycat productions using 60's music as an intrinsic counter-point to the action.

As for us, we used contemporary music when it fit our needs, and opted for classical music when it worked. A tape we made on library orientation for internal use, for instance, opened and closed with *Fanfare for the Common Man*. It fit, both musically and philo-sophically, and we had little worry that Aaron Copland would come after us for using it.

A LITTLE COMPLEXITY

To get back to our editing story, the rest of the school research tape fell into place just as we had shot it, so that there was little, outside of a few insert edits, that took much time or effort. Adding the credits at the end was done carefully, though, to insure proper mention of all those who had helped us to make the program successful, including the students who provided us with those marvelous opening shots.

It's a far different story when dealing with a more complex edit-ing job, such as the tape made about the harbor project. For one thing, many more raw tapes were involved, and much footage was shot over a two-year period that had to be reviewed and reevalu-ated before the final edit could begin. It was annoying to discover that time constraints kept us from getting shots that would have worked extremely well in the finished product. Even more annoy-ing was the fact that we often didn't have footage we were sure had been made. Two years is a long time.

We didn't set a final date for completion of the tape until we found ourselves in a box: a trustee had volunteered our participa-tion in a citywide celebration, and decided that the easiest thing to do for the library's contribution to the entertainment was to show the "harbor tape" that everyone had been asking about.

Since the celebration was less than a month away, we found

ourselves in a bit of a crunch to complete the edit. Luckily, we had
been getting interviews with the major players in this project, and
had only to get a couple more, plus some additional footage, to
begin the process. It would have been nice to have more time, but
on reflection, it also kept us from trying for an impossible standard
of perfection.

One morning when I woke up I heard my clock radio playing a
piece of New Age music, and images began to run through my
head. I bolted out of bed and ran to write down the title. This was
the sound of our harbor tape! I groped for pencil and paper and
listed the name of the album and composer, and set out to buy a
copy of the tape for Barry to hear.

It took a week for my special order to come in at the local mall,
but it seemed more like forever. When I'd raved to Barry about the
sound he was skeptical as usual about my taste, which ran to the
classics. But I felt perfectly vindicated when we slipped that tape
into the stereo player and he heard it for the first time.

Barry's eyes glazed over, and I knew that he was seeing images,
just as I had done. "What would you think," he said, rewinding the
tape, " if right here..." and he played the opening stanzas..."we had
the sun rising over the harbor, and each time the music hits, we
jump cut to a brighter, broader view of the marina, and then..."

I grinned and agreed that it would be great, but we didn't have
any sunrise shots of the marina. "We will," he grinned back. And
within a week he had gone out at dawn to shoot just the perfect
sunrise, had the footage he wanted, and our opening shots were in
the can. All we had to do at that point was incorporate all the
complicated parts: the construction footage, the interviews, and the
narrative, into a coherent, entertaining and historically correct
production. Piece of cake.

MAKING THE HARD CHOICES

One of the jobs assigned to me felt like the hardest part of the
whole process. I had to review all the interview tapes and note
exactly which quotes we were going to pull to fit into each segment. Knowing my packrat mentality, Barry insisted that I had to
be exact and ruthless in my choices. It helped that we had decided
up front to construct a ladder of quotes into a three part story: how
the project came to be conceived and organized; how the actual
construction process looked; and what effect the project had on

future plans for Racine and Racine County.

Using the ladder analogy, I took copious notes as I watched each tape, writing down quotes from each of our participants with an eye to which told the story best at that point, and which carried the story forward to the next point. If two people covered the same ground, I tried to choose the one whose interviews had been used least. In some cases, however, we had to go with one person more than another simply because that person covered more pertinent points than anyone else.

I had to watch those tapes several times, noting where each quote appeared on the raw tape, the exact wording of the opening lines and precisely where I wanted us to cut the quote. This was a real bear; at first I thought I could simply write the essence of a quote and pick it up easily later, but I found that watching it so often had muddied my memory, and I was taking bits and pieces from much longer quotes and condensing them in my mind.

To take a sentence here and a sentence there and meld them together on tape can certainly be done. But it becomes a clumsy piece of work, and requires more cover shots than letting an interview run for the same length of time without all the patchwork quilting. There are times, however, when you can use this technique to make the person on tape look much smoother and more confident by cutting out throat clearing, stutters, or other slight imperfections in the narrative.

It gets to be a judgment call about how much cover will be intrusive, and how much verbal static can be accepted as natural and not worth fussing over. One of our interviews involved a man who spoke rapidly and covered much interesting material; but he stopped to clear his throat often, not leaving a whole lot of time between that sound and the next bit of information. We wound up leaving much of that mannerism in, simply because it would have been too difficult to cut out. When a person speaks quickly, even the best editor in the world will have problems taking out small segments without losing part of the following sound with it.

YOU MUST REMEMBER THIS

There was one experience that taught me a lesson about long-term projects and people's memories. We had recorded interviews with the Mayor and County Executive just before election time, months before the project was due for completion. We needed to do it then, since we knew that the Mayor was not running for another term, and this would be our last chance to hear his version of the project plans while he was still Mayor.

In the case of the County Executive, he was facing stiff competition and there was speculation that he might lose the election, despite his excellent record of service to the county. In fact, he was very candid about that possibility when he granted us an interview, and was gracious and helpful in the process. We got much of our best stuff from him.

In the process of pulling out these quotes, however, I discovered that much of what the Mayor had said, while interesting, was so rambling that it was difficult to find precise quotations to insert into the story. In the end, only two brief quotes out of a two hour interview were actually used. And those quotes had been assembled by the method I described above, from starts and finishes that were sentences apart.

I was in agony. What would the Mayor say when he saw the tape? We had recorded more of him — much more — in terms of time than anyone else involved with the harbor, and yet he barely appeared in the production. I was sure he would be terribly upset.

When I called him to invite him to the premiere, however, he sounded puzzled. "Why invite me?" he asked. "Did I have anything to do with this video?" He had totally forgotten the interview he gave us a year before. I took no pains to remind him of how extensive it was, and concentrated, instead, on telling him about a picture of him that we featured in the tape. When the ice rink at the festival site opened for the first time, with bands and balloon launches, we had gotten some marvelous footage of him skating in his shirtsleeves with a broad smile on his face as the first one around the rink. It was great video.

Don't count on everyone you interview to have such a favorable lapse of memory, however.

When you've gone through the process of editing each segment and have come to a logical, preferably upbeat, ending, it's time to think about the credits you will add to the ending. Barry and I flipped a mental coin some time ago and decided that he would list himself as editor and I would list myself as producer. Whether or not we also added cameraman to his title and writer to mine, those were the two major divisions we agreed on. Mostly, I think it was due to my opinion that "the editor gets the glory and the producer gets the s—."

Parenthetically, this is a good time to mention that when the final credits are laid in on your master and you're sure that it's going to fly, you immediately make a dub of that master to be used as your circulating copy. If anyone else wants to have a copy, fine. But never, under any circumstances, let that master out of your back room.

Well, there is one exception to that rule. You will probably be using your master during a premiere showing if you'll be using projection equipment. A dub will not project as clearly as a master.

But you need to keep that master safe, since you don't want to ever have to edit all your raw tape again. If a circulating dub is lost or broken, you can make another one from the master. But if the master is gone, your only alternative is to re-edit the entire tape from scratch. You may or may not have chosen to keep all the footage from which you made the master, since that gets to be a lot of storage space for used tape. So for all practical purposes, your master is a one-and-only, and should be treated as such.

When your staff has flipped its collective coin to decide on which division of credit goes to which person, it's time to deal with real life issues on the credits. One thing we did as a matter of course was to always put up a slate identifying each project as a copyrighted *Racine Public Library Video Production* with a separate slate for the current City Librarian's name.

This served basically to identify and establish ownership, and it also acted as our bit of gratitude to the administrator for letting us do the work. Different directors have differing attitudes about this issue, however. And you don't ever put anyone's name on a production without letting that person know you're going to do it. The director in charge at the time I left the library, for instance, did not want his name on videos for any reason, so we respected that choice.

You'll find very few people who don't want to see their names in the credits if they had anything at all to do with the production, however. In fact, one of the things you'll be doing with your left hand while making all those other notes with your right hand will be — yes — to make careful notes of everyone involved, with the correct spelling of their names and their correct titles, when appropriate.

In the case of the schoolroom full of students, we compromised by giving them a group "thank you" rather than list 35 separate names; we already had a cast of thousands, it seemed, and didn't want the credits to run longer than the story itself.

But in our harbor video, we were careful to list all the participants, all those who gave us additional footage to incorporate into the production, and everyone who gave us information or technical help. A sincere thank you is that much more sincere when it's in writing and everyone can see it.

SEE HOW THEY RUN

You have complete say over how these credits will run. We generally listed our participants very much the same way a film studio would. The "stars" were identified, then the "bit players" and then the "grateful acknowledgement is made to..." names. Sometimes we'd throw up a slate that said, "Special thanks to ... for their assistance with this production," which covered use of Museum facilities or company hardware or whatever. We always saved the copyright slate for last.

Our single exception to that rule was the Sister Cities tape. In this particular case, the last slate dedicated our production to the memory of a very special man who had been the guiding light behind the whole concept and who died unexpectedly half-way through the taping. We talked it over with everyone else involved, and they all agreed that that should be the last thing people saw on the tape.

There are different ways to put credits on the screen, but the technique we used most was the crawl, putting one or two names and titles up on the screen at a time and then using the character generator to move them upward, just like the movies, until the final slate, kept on screen for several seconds before the tape was over.

The speed of the crawl is purely subjective. If we had a program that was fast-paced and included several people who would be listed in the credits, the movement was fairly brisk, just allowing enough time for them to be read in passing. To be sure you've left enough time, read the names yourself and then add a count of three to it.

If, on the other hand, there were fewer credits to get through and the tone of the video was more sedate, a slightly slower crawl seemed to fit well. One nice thing about doing the crawl at the end is that you've had a chance to adapt to the pace of the tape as a whole; it becomes almost automatic to match that pace with the credits.

The speed is far less important than the contents. More than once, I wound up making phone calls during the process to verify an exact title or spelling of a name. Even when you're sure you're right, it doesn't hurt to check, just in case. People are understandably sensitive about the spelling of their own names or designations. At the risk of boring you with repetition, here's another place where making a habit of listing *everything* can help you out. At the time anyone is added to your cast, or contributes an element to your production, write down all the information you're sure you won't need later. Trust me, you will.

And as you're putting in closing credits, you will also be making some other plans involving those names. It isn't enough to have completed this wonderful production. You have to let people know that you've done it. One of the first things you will want to do, as I've said repeatedly, is to set up a premiere showing.

Invitations can be formally made up and sent out, or you could just pick up the telephone and call the primary people who would be interested in seeing the first viewing of your tape. That's where your list comes in. It's only polite to invite everyone who was involved in the production at any level, and that includes staff members of your library, too.

If you are as lucky as we were, you'll have a place made available to you that's large enough to hold a number of people, has adequate projection equipment to make your tape visible to a large group, and has enough appeal for the general public that it would be a draw in itself. In our case, the Golden Rondelle Theater, operated by SC Johnson Wax, was our haven. The Rondelle was the site of two of our premieres, notably the Vietnamese tape and the Sister Cities tape.

We were able to turn these events into high media coverage, high visibility showings that garnered pictures and stories in the newspapers, made everyone involved feel very good about themselves, and generated a good deal of interest in the tapes mentioned in the papers, as well as in other tapes available through the AV desk. It's rare that you will find an organization willing to put time and money into things of community interest, but the Rondelle not only housed our showings, but designed and paid for newspaper ads and invitations to all the people on our list. Their staff people were incredibly patient and accommodating to us.

In the case of some of the other tapes, we held the premiere showing in our own meeting room and generated our own invita-

tional mailing list. For the harbor tape, we used the festival hall as
an appropriate setting for the story of the how the festival site came
to be built; and in the case of the foster parents tape, the county
social services office opened up their facilities to a very interested
audience.

You can find any number of places happy to cooperate with you
in giving your production a good sendoff and there's more involved in this than just a feel-good exercise in ego. Part of your job
is to let people know what's available to them. A premiere showing
gives you an event, a time-line, that will insure media interest and
also pique the public's curiosity.

Whether it's the AV team that follows through, or if the team
will be working with PR people, it's important that this information
gets the best possible play. Ask for all the cooperation you can
from the people whose site you're using. If they'll provide some
publicity, wonderful. But if not, you must be sure that you do.

For the Humanities funded tape on the Vietnamese, for example, we not only had Rondelle publicity, but the Committee sent
us large, pre-printed posters to use in our informational campaign.
We added our own text to these posters and took them everywhere
we could get them put up. In the case of other productions, we
made up our own posters and distributed them widely. But there
are additional avenues of publicity, and we used them all.

As editor of our library newsletter, I was shameless in giving as
much space as possible to both upcoming and completed videotape
productions. I put in names of staff members participating, anecdotes about the shoot, and in general did a *rah rah* sort of approach,
since the more than 500 people who received the bi-monthly publication were also the sort of people who would be interested in
either attending a premiere or having access to the finished tape
afterwards.

The most basic public notice of all, of course, is the news release.
Since I also wrote the news releases, it was pretty easy for me to
control this aspect, but if you have to deal with another department, follow through to be sure that the releases contain all the
information you need to attract public attention.

WHO, WHAT, WHEN AND WHERE

Check that the time, day and date of the premiere are clearly
noted, and if the general public is invited, as they should be, be up

front in letting them know that there's no fee involved. Give a brief description of the production, making it as interesting as possible. When people read it, it should sound like something they'd really want to leave the house to see. Remember what it was that attracted you to the idea, and use that same enthusiasm to describe it to others.

Make sure that this news release goes to every media outlet in your area: radio stations, newspapers, weeklies, and cable/network television stations. They use these PSMs more often than not, and even if only half of the places solicited give you time or space, you're far ahead of the game. We never had to buy space for advertising our events, which is just as well, on our budget.

Don't forget to mention anyone locally famous who may be involved in the tape. When we had public officials involved, as in the harbor or the foster parents tapings, we put that information up front in the publicity. For one thing, it's a thank you to those who gave you their time, and it's informative for those in the public who want to know what their officials are doing.

One other thing to remember when you're making up that invitation list is that everyone who impacts on your budget decisions should be on it. That includes your administrator, the staff, the mayor, legislators, and key department heads at city hall. It doesn't hurt to put out a general invitation, usually on a flyer, for all other personnel in city departments. While you don't want to give the impression that these events are only for the elite, the decision makers that you deal with not only appreciate a personal invitation, but they're sometimes annoyed if they don't receive one.

Be sure that all those who participated are asked to come, and if they ask you to include other names on your premiere list, do so. It's common courtesy, but sadly enough, it doesn't go without saying.

Don't, by the way, sit down quite yet. If you've gotten out invitations, news releases, flyers and personal phone calls, you've got a good start on the program. Now you have to think about the physical needs involved in setting up a premiere.

Do you have sufficient seating for the crowd you're expecting? While you can't always gauge these things with a high degree of success, you can get some notion of what to expect if you've put an RSVP on your invitations. The response you get from other sources, however, is pure conjecture. If you have something of broad public interest, you may get a larger turnout than usual.

Use your best guesstimate when you can control the seating, and put out fewer chairs than you consider to be your maximum (having some spares close by), since a large space half full provides a far different ambiance than a small space filled to the brim with the same number of people.

You're going to need someone to introduce these events. If possible, try to get someone other than yourself or your staff to do it, since this is a time for words of praise, and it might seen self-serving for you to be tooting your own horn. Sometimes the director will be willing to act as host, sometimes one of the major contributors will do so, and sometimes you just have to handle it yourself.

Remember that the first rule of these events is to spread credit lavishly among everyone involved. Don't be afraid to give public thanks to your hosts, those businesses or groups whose help you needed, or anyone else who might be sitting in the front row waiting for a stroke from you. This is no time to beat your chest and crow, "I did it, it was me, it was me!" Tacky at best, and untrue, as you should have discovered when you did the credits.

When setting up the event, you may choose to serve refreshments, or you may even be lucky enough to have your host provide them for you. Most of the time, however, we didn't, since it would have required more budget and more space, two things we didn't have in abundance.

You can decide how you want to handle it as the event shapes up. The larger the anticipated interest, the more you may want to make it possible for people to mingle afterward, enjoying refreshments and providing you with feedback. Just don't feel underappreciated if someone in your audience informs you that his/her twelve-year-old niece is working on a video just like yours with her little camcorder.

After you've completed a larger body of work, you may wish to do what we did, and design brochures listing all your original productions, along with a special puff piece on the latest creation. These brochures can be handed out at each premiere, but they can also be handouts at the AV desk, branches of the library, and also, wherever you can get cooperation — such as local stores that sell VCRs and related equipment. It's nice to include AV open hours, phone number and any other information that those not familiar with your facilities will want to know.

At this point, you're getting back to the original question: who is your audience? If you have a particular group of people who will be especially interested in the subject at hand, make sure that they receive information about the tape. Flyers mailed to the headquarters or handwritten notes are all you really need to let people know about it.

If you mention that the tape will be available through your AV desk after the premiere, this opens up the possibility of making more people interested in seeing it. Once it starts circulating, word of mouth may keep it going for some time, but it doesn't hurt to keep some of your posters around in the AV office, to remind people — or let them know for the first time — that these videos are available.

While we cataloged them and put them on the shelves just like purchased tapes, we made sure that our own productions were given to patrons without charge, and we often recommended them to teachers looking for supplemental media support for their classes.

Our brochures went to schools, both public and private, so that our productions could be incorporated into the curriculum in whole or in part. The Black history tape, for example, gets a real workout in February during Black History month. It has a certain freshness to it, showing role models in our own community instead of sports and political figures who seem larger than life and therefore out of reach for the students who watch it.

I once went to one of the local elementary schools with the Gilbert Knapp tape, to explain to second and third graders how the tape came to be made, and to talk to them about the history of Racine. I must confess that those little ones really knew their stuff, and even caught me short on some details. The teacher later confessed that they had spent the day before cramming on local history.

It may seem that this is a lot of work to do just for one service that you provide, but if you've been in the business for any length of time you know that it's not possible to keep everyone informed of everything available to them by mentioning it only once. Repetition, especially to each new class of children that comes along and knows nothing about your productions, is the only way to keep your work in front of the public and well used by them.

And by letting the public know what you're doing, you open yourselves to a broader variety of suggestions and information about future production possibilities. Everyone is an expert on something; it may just be that one of those experts will have something worth while to tell you about, but the only way you'll find out about it is to make that person aware of your capabilities.

Making the production can be the most frustrating, exciting, boring, irritating, wonderful working experience you'll ever know. But it's the use that's made of these productions that finally gauges their worth, and it never hurts to beat the drum and let people know that they exist and that they are worthwhile.

And it never hurts to sit back after all the hoopla is over, before the next project is under way, and reflect on what you've accomplished. If your experiences have been normal, you'll have a long list of things that you will do differently next time. But you should also have a long list of things that allow you to sit there with a stupid grin on your face and just feel good. Go ahead; you're entitled.

But if you've reached the stage of being almost ready to release your work and suddenly discover that things are just not going right, you may want to review the next chapter and consider what's involved in putting closure on a production.

Even when you've read all the directions and made all the right moves, there are times, especially when you're new at video production, when you just feel stuck. Don't let it throw you. It's not fatal.

As the saying goes, it ain't over 'til it's over.

SEVEN

The Finished Product:

The Five Stages

Of Closure

POST PARTUM BLUES

If your experience is typical, by the time you're ready to wrap up all those loose production ends, you'll have begun to eye your work with mixed feelings. After all, you've been through a lot. You gave this project all of your attention, your strength and your determination, and now you feel as if you've just put down a heavy load. But somehow you can't seem to okay those closing credits and put it in the box.

It's frustrating. You've worked your way through the spine of the tape, adding all the inserts exactly where you planned to. You've decided that good enough will have to do in a segment you wished had been stronger. You've smoothed the occasional glitch and agonized over the nose rubbing on camera that made additional cover footage necessary for a key interview.

All of this, and you still have a nagging feeling that it's not quite ready. The problem is not necessarily with you or your decision processes. The plain fact of the matter is that it's hard to tell when you're really through.

You are definitely *not* through when you reach the stage (or multiple stages) when you can't stand the thought of looking at it one more time and you'd put anything on tape at that moment just to get it over with. That's battle fatigue, and you've probably experienced it more than once in any long-term production. Take a walk, have a beer, or call your analyst.

When you come back, you'll need to use all of your senses to judge what you've done up to this point. And I'm not just talking about the five senses that we ordinarily think of. Sight and hearing are obviously your primary guides, but you need to stretch the definition of sense beyond the obvious. For example, "pace" can be seen to correspond with your sense of touch, since they both provide you with accurate but hard to define means of nonvisual, nonverbal information. And there is the sixth sense that all good video producers have, that little *ping* in the back of the mind that goes off when something is just right.

RIGHT BRAIN THINKING

I don't mean to fudge on outlining crucial elements of production. I know how important it is, especially to administrative people, for you to be totally factual and straightforward in your evaluation of what you're doing. But this is one of those times when you have to realize that you're dealing with two different paradigms, and what fits into an administration's world of reality is not the same thing as the reality of creation.

It's becoming almost okay these days to be creative, you see. We've come to realize that in addition to those who have verbal skills, and those who have spacial, math-related skills, there are a host of other ways to measure intelligence. If you're looking for a common denominator that will help those around you to understand what it is you're trying to achieve when you produce a worthwhile video, you might try to show the very best examples of classic works to explain what you're up to.

You may have to go into the 16mm collection to show the type of documentary that you have in mind (and it's not a bad idea to review those films yourself to see how the best minds have handled such productions). While film is a different medium, with more subtle shadings of greys and blacks and colors, content can still be compared equitably. You may not have the use of wildly expensive cameras and lenses and lighting effects, but you should have the sense of storytelling, the pacing, and the same wisdom it takes to concentrate on the story and the storyteller, with only as much filler as is necessary to illustrate and complete the tale.

In a sense, you've gone back to the oldest type of human activity, the gathering of the tribe before the communal fire, with facial expressions and voices and gestures recreating an event so fascinating that it needs very little to achieve a hypnotic effect.

That's essentially what your tape should feel like to you, and if it doesn't, you may have to go outside of your own subjective view, using more objective criteria to help you evaluate your product. If you find yourself caught in a vise of frustration and indecision, you need to determine if you really have arrived at the appropriate moment to end your production, or if your senses are correct in telling you something's not right. There are ways to tell the difference. Follow along through these steps and let them help you make that evaluation.

ONE. *Clean your palate.*

When you've come to the end of your editing, walk away. Put that tape in a drawer someplace, and forget you ever heard of it. Don't look at it for at least one full day. A week is better. This is an absolutely essential step to take; you'll regret it if you let anyone talk you into releasing the tape before it's ready. The production must be examined in its entirety calmly and deliberately, and, frankly, that can only be done when you've distanced yourself from it for a period of time.

In the fast-paced world of commercial television, time is a luxury not many producers can afford. The quality of much of our television programming is proof of this. If you want to have a quality product, take the time to walk away from it in order to see it more clearly when you return.

What's happened, of course, is that you've been working with smaller and smaller details for so long that you've become somewhat near sighted. It's impossible to judge pace, story, or the work as a whole until you've been away from it long enough to see clearly, without seams. You're cleaning your palate.

Try to keep this aspect of what you're doing among members of your own crew, however. It's amazing how many volunteers you'll get to "just check the thing out for you." Since everyone watches television, everyone assumes that they know a good production when they see it. It's bad enough that everyone will expect your two-man job to be the equal of television network products. Don't ask a non-pro to judge your work. That way lies madness.

Just assure anyone who asks that you're doing post production work. In fact, that's exactly what you *are* doing. You have to be prepared to let go of the project if you can, which means not thinking about any aspect of it, certainly not agonizing over a jump cut or insert that didn't quite move as smoothly as you had visualized. The absolute best situation calls for your walking away from all such thoughts for as long as you can hold out.

However, if you just can't get your mind off it, settle for doing some other work that has nothing to do with the tape itself. Write down the credits again. Make sure that you have everyone's name spelled correctly. Doublecheck all titles. Go back over all the phases of the production to make sure that everyone who deserves to be in the credits is there, since one thank you is worth a thousand sorry's.

Yes, I know that you did all that when you were putting all the pieces together, but right now you need to think about something else — anything else — besides that tape. Set up the arrangements for the premiere, fuss over the food and drink, address the invitations, or catch up on all that work piled up on your desk before you even think of looking at the tape.

THE LONG COLD LOOK

Finally, when the time is right, and you've done whatever it took to get your mind off the subject, go back and look at it. Watch it in a quiet room. Don't invite anyone else except your immediate creative crew; if you're like most libraries, that'll be all two of you. But remember, this is serious business. You don't want to take any phone calls, and you certainly don't want any drop-ins joining you. Lock the door, if you have to, but make sure that there are no interruptions or comments from anyone else.

Watch it all the way through without interruption. Don't speak any more than you absolutely have to while the tape is running. No one can completely resist a groan or little smug sound if something grabs you, but other than that, keep it down.

You are going to be amazed. When seen as a totality, your production is far more than all those irritating, nitpicky segments you've been agonizing over. You're seeing it as a whole piece, and if you waited long enough before doing this, you're not going to be thinking about the parts that got left out, or the myriad decisions behind what's on screen at this moment. What you're seeing is the actual production, the program that everyone else will soon be seeing. You're going to have some pretty strong emotions welling up right now. When the tape is over, get up and stretch, congratulate yourself on the good stuff and then move on to point two.

TWO. *Don't make snap decisions.*

Don't be surprised if you hate it. Call it post-partum depression, if you want. Call it creative ennui. What you may be feeling right now is related to both those sensations. It's perfectly normal, especially if you've been under a time crunch and have had to rework many parts of the production while fine tuning it.

I was stunned the first time that I experienced this feeling. I thought it was incredible that the parts that seemed so wonderful to me in the process of editing, were, now that I saw it whole, just plain awful. Or so it seemed at the time.

Don't assume that your audience will see what you're seeing. It's highly unlikely, as a matter of fact, because they will judge the total product as they see it, without the benefit — or the handicap — of knowing all the footage that didn't get in or the script pieces that are figuratively lying on the editing room floor.

When you've survived the shock, remind yourself that this is a pefectly normal phenomenon. Then go back and watch the tape again, this time with a pad of paper and a pencil. You're going to prove to you that you did a good job. And if it doesn't seem quite right after the second viewing, then it's time to do some serious checking.

That first time I experienced revulsion at the sight of a finished tape was a good experience for me, believe it or not, because shortly after that it was viewed by others on the staff, and their comments were uniformly upbeat and complimentary. I thought they'd all gone mad, or perhaps were just being kind. But it was then that I realized I'd been mentally putting things in that just weren't there. I was still seeing excised parts of some heavily edited scenes, for instance, or cover shots that would have been wonderful if only we'd had them. It's the same phenomenon when we're asked to describe someone close to us and we suddenly can't visualize them clearly. We've looked at them for so long and with such affection that they've become much more than their bare physical description.

The tape that worked best for us and looked the most like what we expected it to was the Vietnamese program, probably because it was so tightly structured that each segment echoed the style of previous and following segments. That gave us a beat, a rhythm to follow that made the production flow smoothly and easily through.

Well, not easily; I still went through my gyrations about not wanting to cut out all the good stuff. But once we established the first part, and went through the process of choosing selections, partly based on content and partly based on length, the process fell into place and made subsequent portions easier to choose as we reviewed each interview.

The one that probably gave us the most trouble was, oddly enough, the tape we re-edited from our orientation tapes to make a presentation for a staff/board function.

We kept changing our minds about which segments to include; then it seemed as if we were giving much more time to one person than another; and then we found still a third problem. Ironically enough, neither Barry nor I especially enjoy being on camera. Since we were part of the staff, it was only fair that we be included in this thing, but oh, how we balked at actually sitting still for the taping. It was one of the few times we really did identify with all those other staff people who groaned when we would march in with big smiles and a camera ready to give them another chance at stardom.

Because we were uncomfortable with this tape, we found lots of things to growl about while editing, and we were not overjoyed to see the finished product. To this day, I don't know if we've truly overcome our apathy towards it. On the other hand, many staff people asked us to make copies for them to give to relatives, so maybe it had charms that eluded us.

One way to judge how much of your feelings right now is based on your feelings about the tape and how much is based on reality is to sit back and watch the tape with your eyes half-closed so that you're not really focusing on details, but simply noting the color and flow.

Do you get a sense of sameness as it goes by? Is there so little difference from one scene to another that you lose track of time and get the feeling that you're trapped at a particularly boring lecture? Is there so much movement that you think you've gotten a tape of Roger Rabbit by mistake? Or is there just enough of a balance between the two that you feel alert, but not irritated?

Usually when you follow this technique, you discover that the tape is not that bad, after all. Or you may find that there are portions of it that could use a little tweaking up. We'll talk about how to do that as we go further along.

Incidentally, even if you found that you loved the tape, read through the rest of the procedures anyway. You'll understand even better why you loved it when you've finished.

THREE. *Check the script.*

Take the original script and look it over. Yes, I know perfectly well what it looks like now, with segments crossed out, highlighter in assorted colors marking passages, pencil notations all over the edge, mustard smears on the top. . .

Pick it up, just the way it is, and read it. If your production and the script match exactly, it will be a miracle. There are usually profound changes that take place between paper and tape, and that has nothing to do with the skill of anyone involved, from writer to cameraman to actor to editor. There are a lot of reasons for those changes.

Some changes come about because of unexpected opportunity, a chance to get something on tape that was never planned. One such change came to us when we were doing background footage for our expansion tape and discovered the fabulous shot of the mother and child enjoying the atrium in Appleton's public library.

We had gone there to show inviting vistas and low, spacious stacks with airy reading rooms, and instead we found exactly the ambiance we were seeking in an intimate and beautiful moment that had nothing — and everything — to do with the spaciousness of this place. You have to recognize such opportunities, and you have to be open to the changes that they will cause in your carefully crafted script.

Some things change because what worked so well when you put it in the script may not work on camera. We experienced this when we did the Chiwaukee Prairie taping at Parkside. One of the scientists we were interviewing brought some charts and colored maps to illustrate potions of the material.

It looked just fine on our shooting plan, and it even looked okay when we checked it through the lens. But when we put our tape together, we were not really thrilled with the looks of it. It was impossible for us to eliminate the whole segment, but it would have been so much better if we could have taken that material back to our studio and done a proper layout with it. As it was, it looked like exactly what it was: a videotape of someone holding up papers in a high wind.

Finally, some things change because of purely technical reasons, from sound problems to people in the background doing impolite things, deliberately or otherwise.

I've already mentioned one particularly funny episode that happened when we'd been editing the harbor tape for some time and were pretty well through with a crucial segment. Barry had been adding some footage when he let out a whoop that sent me running into the room. He was pointing to the screen on which the master tape was running, and it was hard to tell if he was laughing or crying at that point.

"Look at it, " he howled. "We can't use this part! Just look at it!" So I looked at it, and discovered to my horror, and amusement, that on footage of state legislators seriously scanning the waterways prior to granting approval for the marina project, as the boat on which they traveled passed close to the camera, a key figure was blithely scratching himself in the immortal style of baseball players everywhere. We didn't use it, of course.

Whatever the reasons, you will see changes between your starting concept and what's showing up on the screen. But when the script was first written, it contained the basic theme of the production, with defined or implied elements that carried out this theme. This could be what the *off* feeling is coming from. Is the message still there, or did you lose it?

Is it possible that in the process of cutting out extraneous elements, you also cut out passages that carried a fact, a story, an attitude that contained essential material? Is it possible that you cut something because you thought it was repetitious and actually cut the subject out completely? Or just the opposite, did you leave in redundant quotes without realizing it?

The hardest thing about doing documentaries, instructional or oral history tapes is making sure all the facts are still on the tape, no matter how many times you've heard them or how well known you assume them to be.

When we did the Sister Cities video, it became almost a nuisance to be sure that in editing we didn't cut a remark from any of the children that carried a fact or theme forward. Thanks to some smart taping on Barry's part, most of the dialogue was done more than once, so that in the process of interediting these bits, we could show action and reaction from individuals and also the whole group without losing any of the script. But, again, we had more time and used a more relaxed approach to this particular tape. We could easily have lost important dialogue if it had been rushed, or if we had assumed that everything had been included in all versions of the scene.

When you're working with one camera, as most of you will be, you'll find that it often becomes necessary to shoot scenes more than once, using a different camera angle to show separate elements of the scene. If your actors get confused, or you get involved in technical elements without paying close attention to the dialogue, you can completely lose a line or even a whole segment of a scene without realizing you've done so.

We found a real blooper when we were doing the research tape for Unified. In moving our setup from a focus on the school librarian to one focusing on the kids, we somehow missed taping a key word spoken by the librarian.

We had the kids' reaction to the word, and the librarian's preliminary dialogue, but as we shifted camera angles between those shots we somehow missed getting the word itself on tape. However, we were able to pull the word out of previous takes and insert it over a shot of the librarian's back, looking towards the students' reactions. Very few people ever knew that she didn't actually speak in the version they were seeing.

To use a more fictitious example, you might encounter a situation such as this one: everyone in your home town knows that the XYZ Corporation is the largest manufacturer of widgets in the world, right? It seems boring to reiterate that fact, so you just leave it out, on the assumption that it's common knowledge.

But if your production is any darn good at all, there's a better than average chance that people from out of town will see that tape, and they may not have a clue about XYZ. You have to tell them, directly or indirectly. And you have to tell them why XYZ is in your storyline, and you have to come to a conclusion about what you've presented, because if you don't, your audience will be very angry with you. They have a right to be. You can't show a smoking gun, a corpse, and a fleeing figure and then shrug your shoulders and fade out. Save that stuff for the art houses.

Despite all the best intentions in the world, every time you create a production, you are taking your own perceptions with you. You do have a point of view, and it's best to acknowledge it at once and deal with it. Accept your own prejudices; allow for them, so that when a broader audience sees the finished product, they have all the information they need to form their own mindset, but they also have some idea of where you're coming from. We approached everything we did with the attitude that what we were showing was interesting and had elements about it which would be informative and interesting to other people, too. But we had to be very clear about the fact that our work was not investigative reporting, and it purposely contained few negative elements. A television news team might consider this one-sided, and they'd be right. But if we insisted on the conceit that we were totally objective, we'd only be kidding ourselves.

While you may be using a fictional script to get across your points, remember that you are not working with fiction. Everything has to be factual; it has to have a point to it; and it has to be as visually clear as it can be made to be.

It goes back to the original point of doing something on video in the first place. When you use a visual medium, you must think in terms of pictures, broad strokes that fit the message you're conveying without a great deal of labored discussion to get it across.

This is the ideal, of course. It just may be that talking heads are the only way to carry your particular message. In oral history, it's pretty much a given, unless you have some photos or other means of illustrating the words being said. But in straight documentaries, there should be a way to show what's being talked about, and if you really think in visual terms, you'll find it.

I remember a shot that Barry took at the harbor front. It was designed to illustrate elements of the park which people had donated money to provide. Several items had already been taped to match off-camera dialogue. When it came to filming the turquoise street lamps around the park's perimeter, however, instead of taking a long shot, Barry used the elegant bent neck of the lamp to frame a lakeside view of the park, beautifully. It startled the eye and caught the imagination. Few who saw it were not delighted with it.

That's what I mean by thinking visually.

CHECK THOSE PARTS

Incidentally, make sure you have included all of the message you started out with. You've been so close to it for so long, you may be taking some information for granted that your audience won't understand unless you tell them. Don't leave out any steps in the "beginning, middle and end" process.

There has to be a clear transition between segments, one that tells the viewer exactly what's going on and how you got from this point to that point in the narrative. It's far too easy to leave things out, assuming that because you know how things came to be, you've somehow made that clear to your audience.

For example, in the library service videotape, the narrative shouldn't have been a problem, since we ought to have known how a library operates, what services it offers and which of those services seem most important to individual patrons.

However, we were often surprised when our patrons cited things that we never thought of, things that skewed the script considerably, and not always in an expected way. We assumed that people would be interested in process — how the materials got into their hand; and surprise, they didn't care all that much. What mattered more was the speed with which we could put useful information into a format that they could use, be it reference information over the desk or access to in-depth scholarship sources. It was a learning experience to have input from real people to help us avoid the cliches that might have followed from a script done with actors and compiled totally in-house.

That experience made the final product more useful to our patrons, but it's also the sort of thing you find out by doing. What we thought would work was not always what found its way onto the final version. But you have to go with what works, and luckily, we were able to make our changes up front instead of getting negative feedback afterwards.

By using this approach, we were able to make natural transitions between what we wanted to emphasize and what the patrons actually valued in terms of library service. Then it was easy to break those segments up into service areas — adult reference, children's stories, etc. — and create a natural flow.

When you judge your tape, look for a flow to be as natural as that, with no jarring feeling that someone just hit a gong and we're off in a different direction now.

If you discover at this point that you inadvertently left out a significant piece of information, this is the time to come up with a solution. As you saw in the story about the school librarian, sometimes you can wing it. If you already have something taped that will fill the bill, as we did, wonderful. It means some re-editing, which is never fun, but it will keep your tape from emerging into public view with a great big hole in its premise.

If you don't have any tape that will do the job, you may have to plan on doing a reshoot, a voiceover, or some other method of patching. Since each case is completely individual, each solution will have to be, too; but if the gaffe is large enough, you really have no choice. Re-editing is going to be necessary.

Sometimes a small point can be covered by putting up a screen with text on it at the crucial point, but that's always a last resort. If you have a creative bone in your body, you'll keep in mind that video is for *show* more than *tell*. Is there a non-verbal approach you can use?

For example, if we left out something essential about the XYZ Corporation, it might be possible to incorporate a visual that will get the point across. It could be a pan of their latest annual report to show growth, or a quick shot of the CEO receiving an honor to show prestige, or a shot of corporate headquarters spreading far into the distance to show size — whatever. If you want to depict international activities, for instance, you might use some stock footage of flags from various countries fluttering in the breeze. Two seconds of that can get the message across quite well, and will take minimal time to add as an insert shot.

If you're really up against it, you'll have to re-shoot the narrative to include this information, possibly as a voice-over covered with complementary footage. But be sure that the missing element is something that you can show visually, and that it really is absolutely necessary to the storyline.

We once found ourselves in a spot where we had to show a technology that didn't exist! We needed to show people checking materials out at the circulation desk using automated equipment that wasn't due to be put in for months. To deal with this, we made the assumption that if it's done carefully, a thing can be implied as having happened without actually being seen.

In a segment of the library research videotape made for the Unified School District, we showed our actors rising from a library reading table, gathering up their books, approaching the circulation desk, and then moving on out, arms loaded — without ever showing the actual check-out procedure.

It got us off the hook of showing antiquated procedures due to be changed shortly. Automated circulation computers would completely alter the way materials were handled by the time the tape was released to schools the following fall.

But we honestly didn't think about it until we looked through the lens and realized that we were watching action at the circ desk that would soon be outdated. If you're really trying to confuse people, show them something that doesn't exist anymore!

The odds of something exactly like that happening to you in

your work are slim, but the principle remains. If you know that changes will be made that could be confusing, try to find a way to get around showing them; in this day of rock videos and 10-second commercials, it doesn't take a lot to get your message across without going step-by-step through the whole thing.

Just as we didn't have to show how the students got to and from the library, we didn't have to show every single move they made in the process of their research nor in their checking out of materials. In these cases, the transitions were implied and could be understood as such by the viewers. Keep your basic message in mind and you can eliminate a lot of unnecessary work.

FOUR. *Watch the screen for balance.*

When you scanned the screen with your eyes scrinched up, were you unhappy with the wall of flesh you perceived? Maybe you overdid the talking heads.

Alternatively, do you have so much cover that the audience lost track of who's supposed to be on camera? You gave careful thought to each shot as it went on tape, but in the process of editing, it's possible to break the pattern you set up. In dealing with one small segment at a time, you could forget what you intended to convey at each point, or you could find yourself with nothing pertinent to use as cover while an essential interview goes on and on.

Too late to say you should have thought of cover shots as you went over the interviews; now is when you need to punt. It's rare that you can't get additional footage of whatever cover you need, but if that should happen, now's the time to sit down and make a list of every possible source of alternatives. For example, it's possible to use colored or black and white photos, a variety of maps, portions of stock footage from your own files, or borrowed tape footage from anyone else.

It takes no more than a few seconds of tape to provide the needed break in a long *talking head* segment. Panning a still photo can work as well as anything else. All it really takes is your imagination coupled with an instinct for what works and what doesn't.

OR, DO NOTHING

And there is a time when you just have to leave it alone. You'll get an instinct for that, too, as you create a larger body of work.

You don't need cover for every single second that someone is talking on tape, for instance. Often the expressions and gestures that accompany words add a dimension that no cover footage could.

That's one of the blessings of oral history. When we did the Vietnamese tape, we were not the only ones emotionally stirred by the faces of people telling how it was to survive the war and escape from its horrors. It would have been criminal to cover those expressions with some banal footage simply to provide cover for cover's sake. Balance is what you need, and you'll become acutely aware of imbalance when you watch the tape in full for the first time.

FIVE. *Listen for pace.*

Pace is something different from balance, at least in the sense that I'm using it here. Remember at the beginning of this chapter, I referred to pace as being analogous to the sense of touch? It's a type of sensory input that has nothing to do with sight or sound. Instead, it has to do with rhythm, with the way that the piece moves through time.

If you were a drummer it would be your job to provide the tempo, to help the other musicians to keep the beat, and to carry the rhythm of the piece. As an editor, you are the drummer of your production, and the pace you're testing for grows out of the very substance of the subject.

Let me give you some examples. We cut the tape of the research students to the beat of rock and roll music. The fact that there was music in the background and music was also used as a transition device is not what I'm talking about. I'm saying that the action of the premise calls for fast cutting, fast moving between scenes, and dialogue that is crisp and to the point. If this is not followed carefully in the editing phase, you can't always distinguish what it is, but you know that your project is "off" somehow: sluggish, dragging.

On the other hand, we cut the Vietnamese tape to a slower, more cadenced beat, so that it had a somber, serious feel to it. Keeping it from dropping to too slow a pace was accomplished by raising the beat at each introduction of a new phase of the three-part narrative.

We also subtly raised the beat in the final segment, when the objective of reaching America had been achieved, but there were still problems to overcome. It was tricky, but it worked. The audience was proof of that, as they stayed glued to the screen through the total experience.

It's not always possible to cut to a beat when you're dealing with real life interviews, where the natural pace of each person can be vastly different from the others. You can try, however, to time each segment so that it balances the others.

While it's hardly an exact science, you can gauge the way the edits should be cut by thinking about the type of music you choose to have as a theme piece. If your instincts call for classical music, you can assume a more stately pace than if you reach for rock and roll. If you get into heavy metal, however, I suggest you tone down the script a bit, because no one will live through it.

Pace, in other words, is the heartbeat of your production. Added to the other elements, it carries the theme and the action from the opening shots through the final credits. And once you catch on to the beat of your project, you'll have no problem at all telling when the beat doesn't go on.

This may seem like a lot of backing and filling to get to the point of satisfaction with your work, but it really makes a difference when you analyze your soon to be finished product carefully. Before sending your tape off to meet the public, it helps to know that you've gone over this list and find yourself satisfied.

1. You've taken the time to clean your palate.

2. You didn't make snap decisions or let despair overwhelm you.

3. You've checked your tape for the theme implicit in your script.

4. You've watched the screen for visual balance.

5. You've listened for the beat of your own drummer.

This might be the time to consider if the addition of special effects or text from the character generator will add or clarify elements of the final production. It might be that what bothers you is too much simplicity. Add bells and whistles whenever you feel they will help, with special effects, sounds and action. But remember that you are not competing with the networks. Something less than totally slick is not only acceptable, but probably a lot better in the long run for the type of production you want to do.

The point of creating original video is not to copy what can be seen anywhere on network television, but to fill the gap that exists in recording local events and reminiscences, to bring the medium into reach of the people around you. Whether you concentrate on productions that record historical events or the stories of interesting people, or if you simply want to make useful library- and education-oriented productions, you know now what you're up against, and you know what you can accomplish with a small staff and limited resources. And that's not bad.

I think if you've stayed with me this far, you're probably convinced that this is what you want to do. You have a sober understanding of what can be accomplished, but you also know there's a chance to go over your own head to create something extraordinary. That's great! That sense of excitement is what will make it possible for you to achieve something truly worthwhile.

What you've learned about the potential costs may have brought you down to earth with a thump, or you may be feeling buoyed by the knowledge of how many avenues are open to you now. Either way, any plans to produce original videotapes will rest initially on the determination, hard work and persuasiveness of the people putting the project together.

Success in the long run will rely on such factors as energy level, enthusiasm, time available and administrative support. It also helps to get constructive feedback from the general public, not to mention those people in your home town whose opinions can make the difference in your budget. These factors are so totally individual that only you can decide what weight to give each one when deciding how to proceed.

PEOPLE POWER

If I've put more emphasis on the people than on the technology, it's on purpose, because all the equipment in the world won't do any good if it's not tied to people with talent and a willingness to work hard.

On the other hand, creating these productions is so heady and rewarding an experience that it's quite capable of generating whatever enthusiasm you need to get the job done.

We had a good example of that when we did the foster parents tape. All the people involved, from the director to the actors to the county executive, were enthusiastic about the project and were willing to work long, hard hours to make the production a success. They were high on the experience, and it carried over into long-term friendships all around. The fact that the tape performed useful service for the community was almost incidental to the process.

Consider all the ways that you can use this medium called videotape to achieve your organization's objectives — for teaching, for publicity, for recording of history, for touching everyone around you, and for reaching out beyond the artificial barriers in our society to bring us together. It calls for a careful balance of dreaming and doing, but it is, despite all obstacles, an adventure well worth the effort. Go on out and do it! And by all means, let me know how it works for you.

APPENDIX: A VIDEOGRAPHY OF LIBRARY PRODUCTIONS

The following is a list of titles and brief description of videotapes produced by the Racine Public Library during the years 1981 - 1989. Presented in chronological order.

Children and the Arts in Racine. 28 minutes. Filmed in cooperation with the Racine Children's Theatre, Wustum Museum of Fine Arts and Spectrum School of the Arts, Racine. Pete Rasmussen, cameraman; Pat Kardas, producer. Edited.

A magazine-style pilot program, this "sampler" was done as if prepared for actual broadcast. Three segments included footage of children learning acting, photography, sculpture and related skills. Interviews with the children and teachers fleshed out the basic story line, while a narrator, Lynn Tracy, introduced each element and tied the program together.

Banned Book Week Panel Discussion. 2 hours. Filmed "live" during banned book month observance at the library. Participants included school and public librarians; media representatives from daily and weekly newspapers; and a college student. Mediator: Nancy Elsmo, Head of Adult Services. Filmed by Pat Kardas. Unedited.

A lively discussion of books banned in the past, how banning affects libraries and how the media deals with the issues of censorship and public opinion. Audience participation.

Racine County Library System Conference On Children's Programming in Libraries. Three segments of approximately 2 hours each. Filmed by Pat Kardas. Unedited.

Filmed at the Waterford Public Library, the segments included how to do children's Hallowe'en makeup; a panel discussion on funding children's programs and/or finding volunteers to present them; and a speech by Dorothy Haas, well-known children's author.

Board of Trustees Conference. On-going all day informational conference. Approximately 6 hours. Filmed by Pat Kardas. Unedited.

Department Heads, Administration and Library Trustees met to go over formal presentations of goals and objectives, as well as information about the structure and policies of the library and its departments.

Racine County Fair. Library Participation. Interviews and footage of Racine County Fair activities sponsored by the Racine County Library System to promote library services. Introduced by Lynn Tracy. Filmed by Pat Kardas. Unedited.

Armenian Genocide Commemorative Program. Approximately 2 hours. Filmed by Barry Johnson. Unedited.

Armenian students and guest speakers provide background information on genocidal activities by the Turks early in the century. English and Armenian language, poetry. Introduced by Julie Der-Garabedian.

Juneteenth Celebration. 4-H student instruction. An evening of speeches, talent presentations and related activities was filmed by 15-year-old Black 4-H students using equipment donated for the evening by the Library; instruction was provided on a volunteer basis by Pat Kardas. Approximately 3 hours. Unedited.

Architect Presentations. Architects submitted preliminary plans for enlarging the library. These presentations were videotaped live for later review by the Board. Six presentations over a 3-day period - about 2 hours each. Filmed by Pat Kardas. Unedited.

Library Orientation Videos. (2 versions - Adult Department and all others; and Children's Department and all others.) This 20-minute tape was intended for use by either Adult or Children's services to show what the library departments did behind the scenes. Segments were introduced by each department head, who did voice-overs of staff working in extension services, audio-visual, publications, and technical services. Cameraman, Barry Johnson; producer, Pat Kardas. Edited.

Staff Appreciation Night Video. 10 minutes. An internal version of the above orientation tape, filmed for use at a special staff appreciation evening sponsored by the Board of Trustees. This tape was intended to broaden Board member and employee understanding of the type of work performed by staff members in various departments. Cameraman, Barry Johnson; producer, Pat Kardas. Edited.

Children Found. 29 minutes. A documentary produced in cooperation with the Foster Parents' Program of Racine County. This film shows the work done by foster parents in caring for children whose home lives are disrupted. Original music and script by Matthew Schliesman, with cameo appearances by Racine County officials. Host, Arthur Dexter. Cameraman, Barry Johnson. Edited.

Chiwaukee Prairie; An In Depth Look. 29 minutes. This prairie's unique qualities and its value to our ecosystem are described by noted environmentalists filmed at a symposium at the University of Wisconsin-Parkside. Cameraman, Barry Johnson; producer, Pat Kardas. Edited.

Gilbert Knapp: His Life and Times. 33 minutes. Two actors, Jim and Vi Yorgan, researched and presented a history of Racine's founder and his wife during the city's Sesquicentennial Celebration in 1984. They recreated their performances on videotape with authentic backgrounds provided by the Racine County Historical Society Museum. Cameraman, Barry Johnson; producer, Pat Kardas. Edited.

Library Expansion Promotional Tape. 11 minutes. In an effort to raise City and public consciousness about the need for expanding the library, this tape featured Jill Jensen as a narrator showing crowded conditions, various alternatives, and the solution proposed by the Administration and Board. It was designed to be used in tandem with speakers from the library, but could also stand alone. A corresponding slide/tape production was made to use when video would not be practical. Cameraman, Barry Johnson; Pat Kardas, producer. Edited.

The Many Faces of Racine. 18 minutes. Produced in cooperation with the Racine Sister Cities Organization and the Unified School District, this film stars local schoolchildren as they discover facts about their home town. Jill Jensen plays the part of their teacher, using the Racine Theatre Guild stage as a backdrop.

This tape was produced as a presentation for Racine's sister cities around the world. Cameraman, Barry Johnson; producer, Pat Kardas. Edited.

Public Is Our Middle Name. 18 minutes. Racine Public Library patrons tell about library services and materials they enjoy most in an informative and light-hearted examination of what the library offers to the citizens of Racine. Cameraman, Barry Johnson; producer, Pat Kardas. Edited.

A Trip To Racine Zoo. 30 minutes. Produced in cooperation with the Unified School District, this film goes behind the scenes at the zoo to show schoolchildren how a modern city zoo is run. The tape is used in the Unified curriculum as well as being available through the library. Cameraman/editor, Barry Johnson. Edited.

How-To Origami. 25 minutes. Keiko Skow discusses the history and beauty of Japanese paper-folding as she demonstrates how to make various items and describes how they are used in Japan. Cameraman, Barry Johnson; producer, Pat Kardas. Edited.

Vietnamese In America: The Racine Experience. 40 minutes. This documentary was funded by a grant from Wisconsin Humanities. It features Professor John Neuenschwander of Carthage College, and includes interviews with Vietnamese refugees and a host family living in Racine. Cameraman, Barry Johnson; producer, Pat Kardas. Edited.

We've Come This Far By Faith. 100 minutes. This oral history of Black citizens in Racine includes the life stories of two gospel singers, a Black Muslim and a renowned educator; it also features a rap session by street counselors. Cameraman, Barry Johnson; producer, Pat Kardas. Edited.

Where Do I Go From Here? - 11 minutes. Made in cooperation with the Unified School District, this tape features two Washington Park High School students, their teacher and school librarian as well as the staff of the Racine Public Library. The students, in doing a homework project, demonstrate research methods for

middle and high school students. Used in the Unified curricu
lum. Cameraman, Barry Johnson; producer, Pat Kardas. Edited.

Great Expectations: The Story of Racine On the Lake. 35 minutes.
This tape covers the planning, construction and dedication of
the Racine on the Lake project, encompassing a marina, county
park, festival site and festival building complex. Interviews
with City, County and Downtown Racine Development
Committee planners bring the story to vivid life with videotape
footage showing the construction process. Cameraman, Barry
Johnson; producer, Pat Kardas. Edited.

SELECTED BIBLIOGRAPHY

Technical information:

The Camcorder Handbook, by Gerald V. Quinn, 1987 (PB) ISBN 0-8306-9601-6. Tab Books Inc.
Complete information about camcorders — combination cameras and recorders — peripheral equipment and more. Geared toward home video use.

Getting The Most Out Of Your Video Gear, by Gerald V. Quinn, 1986 (PB) ISBN 0-8306-0441-3. Tab Books, Inc.
Intended for home audience, information about VCRs, TVs as well as cameras and home taping. Illustrated.

Lighting For Location Motion Pictures, by Alan J. Ritsko, 1979. ISBN 0-442-26956-0. Van Nostrand Reinhold Company.
Intended for professional film use; skip the details about film and concentrate on the excellent layouts for lighting. Illustrated.

Portable Video: ENG and EFP, by Norman J. Medoff and Tom Tanquary, 1985. ISBN 0-86729-147-8. Knowledge Industry Publications, Inc.
ENG means "electronic news gathering"; EFP means "electronic field production." These buzzwords describe video work done on the fly and outside the studio, techniques studied in depth in this book. Some of the information is useful, but intended for a large production staff with network aspirations.

Small Format Television Production, by Ronald J. Compesi and Ronald E. Sherriffs, 1985. ISBN 0-205-08455-9. Allyn and Bacon Inc.
Much detail about camera, lenses, some outdated; excellent sections on graphics and sound. Illustrated.

Video Camera Techniques, by Gerald Millerson, 1985 (PB) ISBN 0-240- 51225-1. Focal Press.
Good advice for those totally unfamiliar with video cameras and how to use them. Somewhat outdated technical information. Millerson's books have been used as texts in communications

classes, notably my own.

Video Involvement For Libraries, by Susan Spaeth Cherry, 1980, 1981
    (PB) ISBN 0-8389-0323-1. American Library Association.
Gives a good overview of the way libraries regarded their role in
video at about the time RPL was starting to think about original
productions. I especially enjoyed the remark, "50% of all available
videotaped materials are pornographic."

The Video Primer, by Richard Robinson, 3rd Ed. 1983 (PB) ISBN
    0-399-50698-5. Perigee.
Slightly outdated, basic technical information. Includes a glossary
that might confuse a layperson.

Video Production Handbook, by Gerald Millerson, 1987 (PB) ISBN
    0-240-51260-X. Focal Press.
Wide variety of illustrated how-to information; some British terms
could be confusing.

Working With Video, by Brian Winston and Julia Keydel, 1986. ISBN
    0-8174-6433-6. Amphoto.
Lavishly illustrated in B&W and color, this book describes professional broadcast video, but does it so entertainingly that it deserves to be read for the pleasure it provides as well as incidental
helpful information.

Pamphlets and books on oral history:

Oral History; Columbia Oral Histories Projects, Institute of
    Inter-American Affairs, 1987. Columbia University.

Oral History And The Law, by John N. Neuenschwander, Ph.D., J.D.
    Oral History Association, Denton TX. Pamphlet Series No. 1;
    1985.

Videotaping Local History, by Brad Jolly, 1982. ISBN 0-910050-57-0
    PB. American Assn. for State and Local History, Nashville, TN.
(I include this book because it's one of the few on the subject of
using video rather than aural recording methods. If you read it,
you'll discover that Mr. Jolly and I have vastly different ideas about
the subject.)

Voices, A Guide to Oral History, Derek Reimer, Editor. Province
     of British Columbia, Victoria, B.C. (Ministry of Provincial
     Secretary and Governmental Services, Provincial Archives)
     Sound and Moving Image Division, 1984. ISBN 0-7718-8396-X.
     Illustrated.

Periodicals:

Video Review, Viare Publishing Corporation, New York. Single
     issue price: $2.25.
Best consumer information available; an annual "best products of
the year" issue in December fills you in on test results, prices, new
trends. Also, they were the first to recognize that a good theatrical
film might or might not translate well into a video format in their
tape reviews.
*Alas, VR ceased publication in May, 1992. You may be able to find back
copies with pertinent information in your local library.*

Video Systems, Intertec Publishing Corporation, Overland Park, KS.
     Single issue price: $4.00.
 For professional video producers, technicians and camera operators.

Books on writing scripts:

Making A Good Script Great, by Linda Seger. Dodd, Mead &
     Company, PB. 1987. ISBN 0-396-08953-4.
Linda Seger has put her excellent seminar into book form. If you
can possibly attend one of her in-person presentations, it will
greatly expand the usefulness of this book. While you may not be
writing for the movies, the advice given here translates well into
video work.

The Screenwriter's Workbook, by Syd Field. Dell PB, 1984. ISBN 0-440-
     58225-3.
This book presents a workshop approach to writing scripts and
shows you how to break down scriptwriting into its discrete elements. Great for writer's block and analysis of scripts in process.

ABOUT THE AUTHOR

PATRICIA KARDAS (B.A., Professional Communications, B.A., Management, Alverno College) is presently the Administrative and Programming Assistant to the Director of the Charles A. Wustum Museum of Fine Arts, Racine, Wisconsin. She is also the president of Writers Ink, a communications support company.

From 1981 through 1989, she set up the first video component of the Racine Public Library , where she was responsible for initiating circulation procedures and purchasing commercially prepared videotapes for circulation to the public. She subsequently instituted and carried out videotaped productions through the Library until leaving in 1989. She serves on the Board of the Friends of Racine Public Library.

DATE DUE

Gardner-Webb Library
P.O. 836
Boiling Springs, NC 28017

DEMCO